MORE PRAISE FOR *Comfort Measures Only*

....

"Rafael Campo is one acquainted with the night—in detail. Wrestling with the lives and deaths of patients who are always individuals to him, and with his own personal blend of body and soul, love and guilt, compassion and exhaustion, fighting pain with the magnificent weaponry of language and cadence, in poem after poem he says to us what he cannot say to the man in the bed: 'You're crying, just like me; you are alive.'"—ALICIA OSTRIKER, author of *Waiting for the Light*

PRAISE FOR *Alternative Medicine*

....

"Rafael Campo is an extraordinarily skillful poet: his technique manifests itself in the range of forms he so brilliantly masters. But he is also a poet of gravity and poignant observation. Unlike so many people writing today, he has subjects, passions, and themes that are profoundly important."—SANDRA M. GILBERT, poet and Distinguished Professor of English Emerita, University of California, Davis

"In a style both precise and emotional, playful and earnest, Campo delivers a most extraordinary message: that in writing, in seeing, in remembering, and in being, we embody, simultaneously, the ache as well as the cure."—BRIANA SHEMROSKE, *Booklist*

PRAISE FOR *The Enemy*

....

"Rafael Campo writes tough, questioning, rueful, exquisite, true-hearted poems that resist nostalgia while testing the transformative power of beauty. In perfectly wrought poem after poem, he explores the 'honor' of sacrifice and the breadth of human fidelities. *The Enemy* is surely Campo's best book yet."—ELIZABETH ALEXANDER, Yale University

PRAISE FOR *Landscape with Human Figure*

....

"*Landscape with Human Figure* is a striking achievement. I am moved, as his readers are sure to be, by Campo's wisdom, maturity, depth, heart, and range of experience."—GRACE SCHULMAN

"Not unlike Chekhov, another physician-author, the steady-eyed Campo comes to terms with the darkest of human problems . . . by fusing empathy and clinical accuracy."—FRANK ALLEN, *Library Journal*

"Campo writes restless, worldly narrative poems, often rhyming, that take—and unapologetically engage—the world as it presents itself. . . . [H]is insouciant, call-them-as-I-seem-them descriptions are luminous, addressing the ravages of AIDS, particularly, with care and respect." —*Publishers Weekly*

PRAISE FOR *Diva*

....

"Rafael Campo's rhymes and iambs construct their music against the edgy, recognizable world his poems inhabit: the landscape of birth and of dying, sorrow and sex, shame and brave human persistence—first and last things, center stage in these large-hearted, open, deeply felt poems."—MARK DOTY, author of *Fire to Fire*

"A virtuoso display. . . . Campo is a master of image. . . . His poems are revealing and courageous."—JAY A. LIVESON, MD, *JAMA: The Journal of the American Medical Association*

PRAISE FOR *What the Body Told*

....

WINNER, 1997 LAMBDA LITERARY AWARD FOR GAY MEN'S POETRY

"Rafael Campo is one of the most gifted and accomplished younger poets writing in English. More than that, he is a writer engaged in several of the pivotal struggles/issues of our era, and what he has to say about them is 'news that stays news.'"—MARILYN HACKER

COMFORT MEASURES ONLY

Date: 1/7/19

811.54 CAM
Campo, Rafael,
Comfort measures only : new
and selected poems, 1994-

Comfort Measures Only

NEW AND SELECTED POEMS, 1994–2016

Rafael Campo

DUKE UNIVERSITY PRESS • Durham and London • 2018

Designed by Heather Hensley
Typeset in Garamond Premiere Pro
by Copperline Book Services

Library of Congress Cataloging-in-Publication Data
Names: Campo, Rafael, author.
Title: Comfort measures only : new and selected
poems, 1994–2016 / Rafael Campo.
Description: Durham : Duke University Press,
2018.
Identifiers: LCCN 2018001403 (print)
LCCN 2018008825 (ebook)
ISBN 9781478002062 (ebook)
ISBN 9781478000075 (hardcover : alk. paper)
ISBN 9781478000211 (pbk. : alk. paper)
Subjects: LCSH: Medicine—Poetry.
Classification: LCC PS3553.A4883 (ebook) |
LCC PS3553.A4883 C66 2018 (print) |
DDC 811/.54—dc23
LC record available at https://lccn.loc.
gov/2018001403

Cover art: Joan Fugazzi, *White Nude.*

FOR JORGE
my comfort
my measure
my only

CONTENTS

New Poems

ACKNOWLEDGMENTS

I am very grateful to the editors of the following periodicals, in which many of these poems first appeared, sometimes in slightly different forms: *AGNI*, *American Poetry Review*, *Antioch Review*, *Bellevue Literary Review*, *Boston Review*, *Cura*, *Gay and Lesbian Review—Worldwide*, *Harvard Divinity Bulletin*, *Harvard Medicine*, *The Hudson Review*, *Journal of Medical Humanities*, *Kenyon Review*, *Massachusetts Review*, *The Nation*, *The New Criterion*, *The New Republic*, *The Paris Review*, *Parnassus*, *Ploughshares*, *POEM* (UK), *Poetry*, *Poetry Review* (UK), *Poets .org*, *Prairie Schooner*, *Seneca Review*, *Slate.com*, *Southwest Review*, *Sugar House Review*, *Threepenny Review*, *upstreet*, *Warwick Review* (UK), *Yale Review*, and *Zyzzyva*.

IT IS NOT UNUSUAL, after I've given a poetry reading, for some impossibly young writer from the audience to remark over the post-literary pretzels and Diet Coke, "Wow, your stuff is really depressing." One especially unkind reviewer of my books proclaimed—in a similar but perhaps more impatiently dire vein—"Bad things happen in Rafael Campo's poems." Coming from a fellow poet—and none of us are generally associated with boundless joy, or even middling cheerfulness—his indictment seemed inordinately cruel. Even my devoted spouse counsels me, after reading my latest villanelle about botulism or ode to schizophrenia, "Honey, maybe you should think about lightening things up a bit." Try as I might to take all of this concern to heart, to see butterflies or snowflakes or flowers as more suitable, or at least less foreboding, objects of literary address, I keep finding myself drawn to write about illness.

Like anyone, I cringe at the kind of person who slows down his car at the sight of a roadside accident, craning his neck in the hopes of glimpsing some awful carnage. I fret about television shows like *House* and *Grey's Anatomy* for sometimes making a ludicrous spectacle of illness. I can't stand it when innocent family members solicit advice about their hypertension or cholesterol, because it seems to me there is so much in the world that is more interesting to discuss; I grew impatient even with my endearing grandmother, when she was still alive and would ask me my advice about her blood sugar.

When I feel I'm about to fall ill myself from such constant noxious exposures, I dig out my well-worn copy of Susan Sontag's scathingly sober *Illness as Metaphor.* "My point is that illness is *not* a metaphor, and the most truthful way of regarding illness—and the healthiest way of being ill—is the one most purified of, most resistant to, metaphoric thinking," Sontag says, and I think, "Take *that,* Sharon Olds!" "The romantic view is that illness exacerbates consciousness," she goes on to say, and I crow, "Take *that,* Franz Wright!" What a relief it is to understand illness for what it really is—matter-of-fact pathophysiology; a boring, unpleasant, and decidedly nonrevelatory experience. Illness is a problem for the human imagination only insomuch as we might seek dispassionately scientific methods to cure it while we avoid the inevitably destructive pressures it exerts on our fragile psyches.

Of course, the next morning always comes, and I find myself in my clinic again, the exam room speaking aloud in all of its blatant metaphors—the huge clock above where my patients sit implacably measuring lifetimes; the space itself narrow and compressed as a sonnet—and immediately I'm back to thinking about writing. Soon enough, my patients start to arrive, and the way they want me to understand what they are feeling only immerses me more deeply in language's compelling alchemy: "The pain is like a cold, bitter wind blowing through my womb," murmurs a young, infertile woman from Guatemala with what I have diagnosed much less eloquently as chronic pelvic pain. "Please, Doctor, can you heal me?" I regard her from across the desk and feel grateful for the computer terminal more immediately in front of me, which allows me to type a little medical jargon into my note before having to actually speak to her. "Send her for an exploratory laparoscopy," growls Susan Sontag in the back of my mind, but she's already had that procedure, along with several ultrasounds and Pap smears, innumerable blood and urine tests, a hysterosalpingogram, a colonoscopy, and a trial (ironically) of birth control pills. We have had this conversation before, which I realize is another way of saying we are together part of a narrative, a story. A story in which irony matters, in which understanding metaphor—might her pain be a wordless expression of her deep sadness at her inability to have a child, or perhaps the consequence of some trauma during her journey north she has not disclosed?—seems to have some irrefutable value. Now, I am thinking again about writing, but not a prescription for the pain medication she always refuses; instead, I am thinking about writing a poem like those of Sharon Olds. I am thinking about the metal speculum clattering in the sink while she sobbed softly after I performed her last Pap smear, as if it were trying to reiterate something about coldness and bitterness, or what we hear and can't hear, or pain and abjection.

Perhaps something about this young woman reminds me of my grandmother, herself incurable—and an incurably hopeful immigrant—which only amplifies my narrative impulse. After all, it was my grandmother who first inspired in me a love of stories. Her words were all she could give me of our homeland, Cuba, that exotic and forbidden place, her own unspeakably painful void. My grandmother was afflicted with what seemed an unfair burden of illnesses. Her treatments for her ailments seemed just as varied as the ailments themselves, from the pills she dutifully swallowed each morning— some prescribed to her by doctors, some dispensed out of her friends' personal hoards—to the prayers she recited before her own tiny shrine to the Virgin Mary; from the magical, strange-smelling *potajes* she brewed with roots and herbs that can't be found in American supermarkets, to the sheer will to endure that seemed manifest in her meticulously kept apartment and her constant humming to herself of old Cuban songs. Some of her illnesses were familiar ones, like diabetes and rheumatoid arthritis; others were conditions that were utterly untranslatable from Spanish to English, like the terrible *patatú*, some kind of debilitating nervous attack, or the more insidious but equally awful *retortero*, which could afflict her for weeks, or even months.

Through her experiences, I saw firsthand just how indistinct could be the boundary between the tersely biomedical and the wildly superstitious: for her painful joints she took gold that the rheumatologist prescribed, the same doctor who ridiculed her use of traditional Cuban remedies. As an impressionable child, I marveled at the idea of this precious metal somehow gilding my grandmother from within, protecting her joints from damage by the power of our wonder at it. Decades later, when she finally died of kidney failure induced by the toxicity of what proved to be a worthless treatment for her, I learned the meaning of irony for the first time. If her rheumatologist in his starched white coat could have been so wrong about one form of treatment, maybe he was just as mistaken about the mystical powers of what was prescribed by the *curanderos*, traditional healers, whom he regarded as ignorant savages.

Maybe Sontag's premise that illness is mere pathophysiology, to be explicated only biomedically, is not an entirely correct notion either; perhaps illness is a kind of muse, luring us to acts of the imagination and gestures of language that have positive effects on our hearts and minds. Song delighted my grandmother, and prayer consoled her; her joints seemed to move freely again when she danced a merengue, or when she knelt her large form before *la virgencita*. No wonder I have come to believe in the power of the imagination if not to cure, then to heal.

Yet still I resist the urge to write. I scold myself for my prurience. I question whether I might be too glib or too sentimental. I agonize over my stake in the telling. Illness may be a muse, but it is a particularly vexing one. I suppose at the root of any act of narrative lies some inchoate desire to bear witness, to say, "I was there," to join with others in a signal experience. When that signal experience is illness, this empathetic impulse seems all the more overpowering, as if some deep survival instinct were triggered, as if we might share in the discovery of some profound knowledge we need to live. If the sensational can thus give way to wisdom—even as we are shocked, we are at the same time comforted—so too can sentiment be supplanted by genuine emotion. Surely we must feel moved by the plight of illness, lest we fall into one of the very traps of specious narrative that Sontag bemoans—when illness strikes, it is not because we are guilty or deserve it, and our defenselessness stirs in us the compassion we feel for the innocent, the underdog, the fighter. How much I want to help my Guatemalan patient; how acutely did I wish I could alleviate my grandmother's pain! When I write about them now, I recall the joke in my heavily seasoned Latino-Italian family that if you're not screaming or crying when you say something, then you don't really mean it, so I must defeat my inborn tendency to exaggerate or to pity, but still I must write, in order to restore, to make sense, to heal.

And to be restored and healed myself—yes, I must also admit my complicity in these stories, that I cannot subtract myself completely from them. Sometimes I discover that I'm really writing about myself, my own arrogance or vulnerability or alienation, and I wonder if what feels like selfishness is at the same time an expression of the familiar wish to identify with another person, to affirm that I'm no different, that I'm equally as flawed and conflicted and needy as any of us is. Illness is, after all, one of the few truly universal human experiences; to write in response to it necessarily demands active participation, not the kind of objective, soulless distancing so many doctors practice, and teach their trainees to practice. To write about illness, to heed this terrible muse, is to reject distancing and to embrace empathy, for which there is no reward or claim on greatness other than perhaps the perverse joy of recognizing oneself as being susceptible to the same foibles and neuroses as anyone.

To write explicitly about one's own illnesses risks an even worse self-indulgence—bunion surgery and hemorrhoids, no matter how distressing to the otherwise healthy poet, simply cannot make for scintillating verse. On the other hand, to write about another's suffering can seem entirely presumptuous, as if it were somehow possible to re-create on the expanse of the clean, neat white page the image an anorexic teenager sees of herself in her bathroom mirror that leads her to induce vomiting—or worse, that somehow, in the earnest imaginative quest for that universal balm that heals, anorexia becomes indistinguishable from anemia; AIDS and ALS and AML, interchangeable.

While it's true that the screams of pain coming from the room in the ER where a woman is losing her baby are no more or less heart-wrenching than those from the woman in the next room who is withdrawing from heroin, the specific details of each story must matter just as much as the ultimately indescribable anguish they share. "We do not know our own souls, let alone the souls of others," declared Virginia Woolf, in her indelibly humane essay "On Being Ill"; though she brilliantly defended the notion of illness as a motive for writing, she too was forced to consider our myriad limitations as our own bodies' reporters. Yet we must rely on these faulty accounts, perhaps taking additional solace in their imperfections, because to do without them would be injurious to the soul, and to not forgive them would leave us utterly hopeless.

The true cynic who exceeds Sontag in her disdain for our silly superstitions and inane hopes will complain that regardless of who gets to tell the story of illness, the patient still feels like crap and wants to be either cured or healed, whichever will bring relief soonest and, in these days of limited resources, for the cheapest price. Meaning for him equals results, plain and simple. Illness isn't a fanciful narrative to him, nor is it the intellectual intrigue of biology gone awry. It is merely some skilled technician's job to fix before moving on to the next illness, a transaction about which no one need care, an occasion for money to change hands for services rendered as efficiently as possible. Stendhal and Sontag, Olds and Woolf mean next to nothing to him—and even less as the surgeon stands poised to make his first cut, or as the oncologist starts the chemotherapy drip. He refuses to consider that even in the immediacy of some critical therapeutic act, he is hemorrhaging his unspoken words. In summarily stapling shut his figurative wounds, he is compromising his best chance at survival by denying himself access to all the possible modalities by which the physician might intervene.

His is an expression, perhaps, of the same overconfidence in the scientific model of illness that Sontag glorified. While Sontag was right to denounce the negative metaphors we concoct out of the same ingredients my grandmother used in her more humane and optimistic responses to her illnesses—thanks to Sontag, as well as to other writers she might have disparaged, like Sharon Olds and Franz Wright (or Mark Doty and Lucia Perillo, or Marilyn Hacker and Audre Lorde, or Alicia Ostriker and Adrienne Rich), we simply can no longer view illnesses like cancer and AIDS as being caused by our fears and our anxieties—we just as adamantly must reject a conception of illness that relies entirely on biomedical definitions.

I am reminded of one of my residents, who was called to run a code on a patient of hers in the hospital just as she was about to leave for the day and enjoy some time with her young family at home. She had followed all the biomedical protocols and algorithms perfectly, barking orders to the nurses and interns with all the confidence she could muster; however, like most end-of-life interventions in the hospital, this one too proved futile, and the patient died. It was only weeks later, when she had the chance to write about the experience (in a poem she created for a reflective writing group that is now part of the residency curriculum in our hospital), that she felt she could do justice to the entire experience, aspects of which she purposefully had shut out at the bedside in the perceived acuity of the situation. Perhaps most salient of all that she had sacrificed to the biomedical exigencies of the moment was the tuning out of the family who were present in the room; she wished she hadn't ignored them, but instead had allowed them to stop her before a full thirty minutes had passed, when it was already amply clear to them that their mother was dead.

It is precisely situations like these that have so long been cited by medical educators as a primary reason for teaching distancing to medical trainees: to be able to function in an emergency, one cannot regard that patient as a whole person, but rather must focus on the malignant arrhythmia or the life-threatening electrolyte imbalance in order to implement the appropriate technologies and in turn save life at all cost. Narrative has no place here, many would argue; we must not be distracted by the color of her nail polish, or the slack blood pressure cuff that hung down around her wrist like some horrible bracelet, or the wails of her children—all details my resident had absorbed in spite of her conscious effort not to register them.

Yet, if we begin to enlarge the context, as narrative asks that we do, if we start to consider that our actions have impact on others who have their own relationship with the person we see exclusively as "a patient" (and not as "a mother," as her children do; not as "a suffering soul," as the chaplain does), we might behave differently. We might move to comfort the patient and to protect her dignity in her last minutes on earth; we might seek to console her children as they face a tremendous loss; we might pray together with the chaplain in the hopes that she not die without the last rites that are soul-saving in many religious traditions. Whether storytelling has a place here is worth considering very deeply; it certainly proved indispensable after the fact, and the poem written by the resident, who was unable to resuscitate her patient in the hospital, perhaps has done her an even greater service, by immortalizing her.

None of us lives forever. Many of us might have our lives prolonged by biomedical interventions whose financial costs are exorbitant; too infrequently do we question the toll they also exact on our humanity. The fantasies about what causes illness that Sontag railed against (cancer results from repressed anger; AIDS is a punishment from God) have been replaced by even more deluded fantasies that science somehow can prevent death. The only way we can defy our own mortality is through acts of the imagination, by creating the stories and sculptures and paintings and poems that will outlast us, but that will always be animated by our will to have created them. Even our greatest scientific discoveries can be understood in this way: they are not truly ends in themselves, by which we can ever hope to explicate away our suffering, but are rather part of the same process of dreaming and desiring, wishing and wondering.

When I visited my grandmother in the hospital in the last weeks before she died, I cried for a while into her shoulder. But by then I was a young doctor, so soon I headed for the nurses' station and pored over her hospital chart while she lay propped up in her bed, the glass-and-metal ICU like the internal workings of some incomprehensible machine designed for time travel. Countless hours and hundreds of thousands of dollars had gone into the attempt to transform me from a long-term financial burden on my parents to someone with a respectable, moneymaking career. She was in heart failure despite being on dialysis, and I tried desperately to understand her fluid imbalances. Her I's and O's were dutifully tabulated, in a sequence that suggested a code whose rules I might decipher. In my exasperation, I looked up from the record of her gradual demise and caught a glimpse of her as she fingered her rosary, praying to herself with a peaceful smile on her face, taking her own measure of her receding life. When I write about her now, all the data that seemed so important then have faded to insignificance—but it is that one cherished detail in my memory, this one little story, that always makes her come alive to me again.

FROM *The Other Man Was Me*

(ARTE PÚBLICO PRESS, 1994)

El Curandero

I am bathing. All my grayness—
The hospital, the incurable illnesses,
This headache—is slowly given over
To bathwater, deepening it to where

I lose sight of my limbs. The fragrance,
Twenty different herbs at first (dill, spices
From the Caribbean, aloe vera),
Settles, and becomes the single, warm air

Of my sweat, of the warmth deep in my hair—
I recognize it, it's the smell of my pillow
And of my sheets, the closest things to me.
Now one with the bathroom, every oily tile

A different picture of me, every square
One in which I'm given the power of curves,
Distorted, captured in some less shallow
Dimension—now I can pray. I can cry, and he'll

Come. He is my shoulder, maybe, above
The gray water. He is in the steam,
So he can touch my face. Rafael,
He says, I am your saint. So I paint

For him the story of the day: the wife
Whose husband beat purples into her skin,
The jaundiced man (who calls me Ralph, still,
Because that's more American), faint

Yellows, his eyes especially—then,
Still crying, the bright red a collision
Brought out of its perfect vessel, this girl,
This life attached to, working, the wrong thing

Of a tricycle. I saw pain—
Primitive, I could see it, through her split
Chest, in her crushed ribs—white-hot. Now,
I can stop. He has listened, he is silent.

When he finally speaks, touching my face,
It sounds herbal, or African, like drums
Or the pure, tiny bells her child's cries
Must have been made of. Then, somehow,

I'm carried to my bed, the pillow, the sheets
Fragrant, infinite, cool, and I recognize
His voice. In the end, just as sleep takes
The world away, I know it is my own.

from Song for My Lover

XI. A MEDICAL STUDENT LEARNS LOVE AND DEATH

The scalpel finds the heart. The heart is still.
The way it rests, suspended in his chest,
It seems a fruit unharvested, its flesh
Inedible but oddly tempting—swelled
A size I never will forget. My sleeves
Rolled up, I touch, I trace an artery—
A torturous, blockaded road—and free
The muscle from connective tissue sheaths
An unforgotten lover left in place.
My working hands become the fluttering
He must have felt; the lost anatomy
Of his emotions, gardens left in haste.
Past human bodies, no one has evolved.
With these deflated lungs, he's penitent,
He wants to say how love will never end.
I cut, and make from him the grave I rob.

XIII. TOWARD CURING AIDS

I slap on latex gloves before I put
My hands inside the wound. A hypocrite
Across the room complains that it's her right
To walk away—to walk away's her right
As a physician. Lapidary, fine,
My patient's eyes are overhearing her.
He doesn't wince. His corner bed inters
Him even now, as she does: he hasn't died,
But he will. The right to treatment medicine
Denied is all the hollows here: along

His arms, the hungry grooves between the bones
Of ribs. As if her surgeon's thread through skin—
The rite of obligation overdue—
Could save him now. I close the wound. The drain
Is repositioned. Needles in his veins,
I leave him pleading. There's too much to do.

Aida

I've never met the guy next door. I know
He's in there—mud-caked shoes outside to dry,
The early evening opera, the glow
(Of candlelight?) his window trades for night—

I think he's ill, since once the pharmacy
Delivered his prescriptions to my door:
Acyclovir, Dilantin, AZT.
He doesn't go out running anymore.

I've heard that he's a stockbroker who cheats
A little on his taxes. Not in love,
They say—he seems to live alone. I eat
My dinner hovering above my stove,

And wondering. Why haven't we at least
Exchanged a terse hello, or shaken hands?
What reasons for the candlelight? His feet,
I'm guessing by his shoes, are small; I can't

Imagine more. I'd like to meet him, once—
Outside, without apartments, questions, shoes.
I'd say that I'm in love with loneliness.
I'd sing like candlelight, I'd sing the blues

Until we'd finished all the strawberries.
We've never met, and yet I'm sure his eyes
Are generous, alive, like poetry
But melting, brimming with the tears he cries

For all of us: Aida, me, himself,
All lovers who may never meet. My wall—
As infinite and kind-faced as the wealth
Of sharing candlelight—it falls, it falls.

The Test

Singing to himself, waiting for the voice
To call him next, he thought it out again.
He was just an accident. As a boy,
He knew there would be awful things, the men
In hot showers suspecting it was true,
His brothers never loving him again,
A balding man, alone, having Campbell's soup
For dinner. But it wasn't until after when
He'd had the surgery, and then in college
The only love he cared about, that he heard
About the virus. He'd had blood, an acknowledged
Several units—but only that one real love—sure,
There'd been some girlfriends too, two or three . . .
He laughed to himself. And doctors were surprised to see
The virus, deadly, in the tears. Where else would it be?

Allegory

Outside somewhere, beneath an atmosphere
So pure and new each breath is musical
And silent, mouth-watering, without taste,
So full of butterflies one can't imagine
Because it hurts to be so free, out there

There was a hospital where AIDS was cured
With Chinese cucumbers and royal jelly,
With herbal medicines, vaccines, colostrum.
I went there in a submarine, through space
It seemed, and I was armed with nuclear

ICDMS. I read the *New York Times,*
That's how relaxed and skeptical I was;
I sat upon the floor, my back against
The gleaming missiles. Strangely, no one else
But me was on the submarine, except

The president, whom I'd confined beneath
The lowest deck, inside somewhere where air
Was scarce and hardly breathable. One can't
Imagine what it's like to see a world
Like theirs from such a distance for the first

Time: God, was it beautiful, butterflies
And silent musical wind, the hospital
Where no one paid. I tried to give them small
Pox, missiles, blankets; they looked at me
Like I was crazy, and they asked me why

The president had been incarcerated.
There's no explaining of morality
To savages, I thought. And though it hurt
To leave, to conquer them and take with me
The royal jelly and colostrum, when I aimed

My missiles at their hospital I felt
Much better. Munching on a cucumber,
The light of the explosion brightening
My face, I couldn't help the tears, I was
So sad and happy, all at once, again.

Age 5 Born with AIDS

In Jaime's picture of the world, a heart
As big as South America shines out,
The center of the only ocean. Three
Stick figures (one is labeled "me") are drawn
Beside the world as if such suffering
Could make us more objective. Jaime's bald
And has no mouth; his parents aren't like him,
They're all red lips and crazy yellow hair
And grins. There is no title for his work
Of art, except the names we give ourselves.

Technology and Medicine

The transformation is complete. My eyes
Are microscopes and cathode X-ray tubes
In one, so I can see bacteria,
Your underwear, and even through to bones.
My hands are hypodermic needles, touch
Turned into blood: I need to know your salts
And chemistries, a kind of intimacy
That won't bear pondering. It's more than love,
More weird than ESP — my mouth, for instance,
So small and sharp, a dry computer chip
That never gets to kiss or taste or tell
A brief truth like "You're beautiful," or worse,
"You're crying just like me; you are alive."

The Distant Moon

I.

Admitted to the hospital again.
The second bout of pneumocystis back
In January almost killed him; then,
He'd sworn to us he'd die at home. He baked
Us cookies, which the student wouldn't eat,
Before he left—the kitchen on 5A
Is small, but serviceable and neat.
He told me stories: Richard Gere was gay
And sleeping with a friend of his, and AIDS
Was an elaborate conspiracy
Effected by the government. He stayed
Four months. He lost his sight to CMV.

II.

One day, I drew his blood, and while I did
He laughed, and said I was his girlfriend now,
His blood-brother. "Vampire-slut," he cried,
"You'll make me live forever!" Wrinkled brows
Were all I managed in reply. I know
I'm drowning in his blood, his purple blood.
I filled my seven tubes; the warmth was slow
To leave them, pressed inside my palm. I'm sad
Because he doesn't see my face. Because
I can't identify with him. I hate
The fact that he's my age, and that across
My skin he's there, my blood-brother, my mate.

III.

He said I was too nice, and after all
If Jodie Foster was a lesbian,
Then doctors could be queer. Residual
Guilts tingled down my spine. "OK, I'm done,"
I said as I withdrew the needle from
His back, and pressed. The CSF was clear;
I never answered him. That spot was framed
In sterile, paper drapes. He was so near
Death, telling him seemed pointless. Then, he died.
Unrecognizable to anyone
But me, he left my needles deep inside
His joking heart. An autopsy was done.

IV.

I'd read to him at night. His horoscope,
The *New York Times*, *The Advocate*;
Some lines by Richard Howard gave us hope.
A quiet hospital is infinite,
The polished, ice-white floors, the darkened halls
That lead to almost anywhere, to death
Or ghostly, lighted Coke machines. I call
To him one night, at home, asleep. His breath,
I dreamed, had filled my lungs—his lips, my lips
Had touched. I felt as though I'd touched a shrine.
Not disrespectfully, but in some lapse
Of concentration. In a mirror shines

The distant moon.

Finally

Two lovers met. It wasn't lovers' lane,
But a lesser traveled road. No others came.
One lover held the other's hand. The other
Man was me. I watched as if I hovered
Far above the scene. And as the sky
Began to prickle with the stars, I tried
To understand why the other couldn't free
His heart the way the birds imperceptibly
Flew, searching for their nests. The first one said
Some words. I couldn't hear, because I bled
So loud internally—a roaring
That might never drain me, a liquid pouring
Itself out. One lover stooped, unlaced his shoes,
And dropped his lover's hand. His clothes were strewn
All throughout the reeds. They glowed like ghosts
Of lovers who had died before. Upon their throats,
The moonlight's touch was particularly white.
One lover held the other's cock. Slow, tight,
His palm confused me with sensation,
Because a lover was the one location
I had never been to. But this man knew.
And as the other's destination grew
Clearer and clearer, like finding the moon
From behind a once-obscuring cloud, the tune
Of its light all at once familiar—
So this is where the lovers came the years
I read about in school. This is always where
They came, from London-town, or county fairs.

I then imagined all the things that the earth
Hadn't held: organ music, in the hearth
Leaping flames, soul-mating, satellites—
Two lovers met. The other man was me that night.

FROM *What the Body Told*

(DUKE UNIVERSITY PRESS, 1997)

Route 17

Just after I had landed my first job—
they needed busboys at the Mexican
chain restaurant that opened where Lake crossed
Route 17, an intersection known
in town for being dangerous—we met.
Among my new responsibilities
was polishing the silverware, he said
while pointing a dull butter knife at me.
He plunged it in a pitcher full of seltzer,
and for a moment it was diamond-jeweled
in carbonation, like some priceless dagger
belonging to a king.
                I wasn't fooled.
His muscle shirts and dancing skills combined
suggested his were pleasures of a sort
not more sophisticated, but *sublime*—
a word I memorized expressly for
the SATs. I planned to go away
to college—Massachusetts, maybe Maine,
which seemed as far away from Jersey as any place
could be. My parents didn't have the means
to pay the huge tuitions, so I had
to work. The friends I made, including Al,
agreed: what I needed to get ahead
was words.
           He also managed a motel
for extra cash. He teased the waitresses;
the constant flirting reassured me. One
named Abby—poverty had made her wise,
at least to me, enamored of the green

tattoo inside her arm—suspected it.
Her ex and her best friend together formed
a band (they called themselves The Opiates)
which played at local clubs and senior proms
until they shocked her with the truth. "All queers
are obvious to me," she told me as
I kissed her tiny freckled breasts, unsure
of my performance.

                          Al was somewhere else
The night I got so drunk I could have done
whatever I imagined he might want
me to. They poured me Cuba Libres, rum
so sweet it made me want to stay, not quit
and go to college. Abby whispered in
my ear, her lips as thick as fingers: "Stay
with me." I wondered why he looked so thin.
I'd noticed how his clothes were ruffled by
the wind as he crossed 17 to get
his car; they seemed a size too big. Unclear
on who I was, I wanted him. "Forget
him, look at me," gnawed Abby on my ear.
I did.

          Just three months later, Al was dead.
It was the spring of 1983,
before the shuttle with the astronauts
exploded. When I took the SATs
I thought of him, the night we saw that wreck
on 17. Six drunken teenagers
from town had crashed head-on into a truck.
Before the ambulance arrived, I heard
Al calling to them, darting underneath
the traffic light, the whole world stopped around
him. Trying crumpled doors, the oily heat

of radiator steam released, he found
their broken bodies first.
                    On 17,
he must have been infected; most rest stops
along the highway to New York were scenes
for cruising. Bodies pressed to bodies, cops
with flashlights peering into cars—today
it seems less glamorous to me. Back then,
the new disease that ravaged Al—("I'm gay,"
he finally confessed, above the din
of Happy Hour in the mirrored bar
as I was finishing my shift. "You need
a ride somewhere?" I hurried to my car . . .)—
seemed so momentous, meaningful as blood.
I wished I had been brave enough, for him;
today, the words I've learned seem guarded, grim.

Prescription

We need more drugs. For cancer, with its claws.
For coronary artery disease,
The elephant that sits upon our chests.
For AIDS. For multiple sclerosis too.

We need more drugs, the kinds that obviate
Sharp needles in our veins. The kinds of drugs
Like nitroglycerine beneath our tongues,
The chants of tribal elders, shark fin soups:

We need more drugs for AIDS. The ampules, clear,
Enough for everyone. No side effects.
No clenching quilts until an isolate
Drips out. No blood. For cancer, heart disease;

For multiple sclerosis, AIDS. It's true,
We might make poetry superfluous.
It's true we might become addicted, but
We'd blame ourselves before society,

We'd blame the blood supply, our genes. We'd need
More love, have greed to spare. There'd be no AIDS;
Instead of money, health care bills get paid
In brightly colored pills that make us dream

This dream: we're insured to the hilt in a world where heart
Disease is curable, where poetry
Was all we ever needed to cure AIDS,
Where victims, all of us, are innocent.

The Good Doctor

A doctor lived in a city
Full of dying men and women.
He ministered to them
A medicine admittedly

Not curative, and only
Slightly toxic. The medicine
Was known as empathy. It worked
Until the doctor grew more lonely—

His patients only died less quickly—
And in a fit of rage
He burned its formula.
Word spread to the sickly

As the virus had: precise
And red, omitting nothing.
The doctor's reputation changed.
No longer was he viewed as wise;

Instead, when patients came
To him they brought suspicion;
They held their breath when he would try
To hear their songs. His names,

Once various and musical,
Were soon forgotten.
When he died of the disease,
They left him where he fell.

She states that things at home are fine.
On physical exam, she cried but was
Cooperative. Her abdomen was soft,
With normal bowel sounds and question of
A suprapubic mass, which was non-tender.
Her pelvic was remarkable for scars
At six o'clock, no hymen visible,
Some uterine enlargement. Pregnancy
Tests positive times two. She says it was
Her dad. He's sitting in the waiting room.

V. JOHN DOE

An elderly white male, unresponsive.
Looks homeless. Maybe he's been here before:
No chart. No history. His vital signs
Were barely present, temperature was down
Near ninety, pressure ninety over palp;
The pulse was forty, best as they could tell.
They'll hook him to a monitor before
They warm him up. I didn't listen to
His lungs—I bet I'd hear a symphony
In there. I couldn't check his pupils since
His lids were frozen shut, but there were no
External signs of trauma to the head.
They found this picture of a woman with
Two tiny kids still pinned inside his coat.
It's only three AM. The night's young. If
He's lucky, by tomorrow he'll be dead.

VI. S.W.

Extending from her left ear down her jaw,
The lac was seven centimeters long.
She told me that she slipped and struck her face
Against the kitchen floor. The floor was wet
Because she had been mopping it. I guessed
She'd had to wait for many hours since
The clock read nearly midnight; who mops floors
So late? Her little girl kept screaming in
Her husband's thick, impatient arms: he knocked
Three times, each time to ask when we'd be done.
I infiltrated first with lidocaine.
She barely winced, and didn't start to cry
Until the sixteenth stitch went in and we
Were almost through. I thought my handiwork
Was admirable. I yawned, then offered her
Instructions on the care of wounds. She left.

VII. MANUEL

In Trauma 1, a gay Latino kid —
I think he's seventeen — is getting tubed
For respiratory failure. "Sleeping pills
And Tylenol," I translated for him
As he was wheeled in. His *novio*
Explained that when he'd told his folks about
It all, they threw him out. Like trash. They lived
Together underneath the overpass
Of Highway 101 for seven weeks,
The stars obstructed from their view. For cash,
They sucked off older men in Cadillacs;
A *viejita* from the neighborhood

Brought tacos to them secretly. Last night,
With eighteen-wheelers roaring overhead,
He whispered that he'd lost the will to live.
He pawned his crucifix to get the pills.

VIII. F.P.

Another AIDS admission. This one's great:
They bring him in strapped down because he threw
His own infected shit at them—you better bring
Your goggles!—and a mask, we think he's got
TB. He's pissed as hell. Apparently,
He wants to die at home but somebody
Keeps calling 911. A relative
Back home in Iowa, or some damn place.
Just keep him snowed with Ativan—believe
You me, you do not want to get to know
This fucker. Kaposi's all over, stinks
Like shit—incontinent, of course. How long
Before you get down here? Because his nurse
Is driving me insane. Of course we got
Blood cultures . . . yeah, a gas—OK, I'll stick
Him one more time. The things you do for love.

IX. TOMMY

A twenty-one-year-old white man brought in
By ambulance—in hypotensive shock,
Shot in the back while buying drugs from three
Black men. The cord must be involved:
His legs are paralyzed, his penis is
Erect, and all sensation from below
The level of the entry site is lost.

They left him in the street for dead; I heard
Them say an alley dog was lapping up
His blood like milk when he was found. Before
He goes to surgery, he has to give
Informed consent, which he's refused to do
Thus far. He states he'd rather die than be
Dependent on his family for care.
They're questioning his competence, of course.
They're waiting on his folks. His wife just stares.

X. MARIA

This G2, P1 gives us a confusing
History. It sounds like she's been pregnant
Approximately thirty weeks, although
She can't recall her LMP. No pain,
But bleeding for about two days. Of course
She hasn't had prenatal care, and God
Only knows where the father is. She works
Two jobs that keep her on her feet all day.
She's been in the United States six months,
And doesn't speak a word of English. Bet
You she's illegal. Cervical exam
Is unremarkable, the os is closed.
I think we need an ultrasound to tell
Us more. Besides a look at the placenta,
We need some confirmation of her dates.
Her uterus can tell us more than she can.

XI. JANE DOE #2

They found her unresponsive in the street
Beneath a lamplight I imagined made
Her seem angelic, regal even, clean.
She must have been around sixteen. She died
Who knows how many hours earlier
That day, the heroin inside her like
A vengeful dream about to be fulfilled.
Her hands were crossed about her chest, as though
Raised up in self-defense; I tried to pry
Them open to confirm the absence of
A heartbeat, but in death she was so strong,
As resolute as she was beautiful.
I traced the track marks on her arms instead,
Then pressed my thumb against her bloodless lips,
So urgent was my need to know. I felt
The quiet left by a departing soul.

Lost in the Hospital

It's not that I don't like the hospital.
Those small bouquets of flowers, pert and brave.
The smell of antiseptic cleansers.
The ill, so wistful in their rooms, so true.
My friend, the one who's dying, took me out
To where the patients go to smoke, ivs
And oxygen in tanks attached to them—
A tiny patio for skeletons. We shared
A cigarette, which was delicious but
Too brief. I held his hand; it felt
Like someone's keys. How beautiful it was,
The sunlight pointing down at us, as if
We were important, full of life, unbound.
I wandered for a moment where his ribs
Had made a space for me, and there, beside
The thundering waterfall of his heart,
I rubbed my eyes and thought, "I'm lost."

My Voice

To cure myself of wanting Cuban songs,
I wrote a Cuban song about the need
For people to suppress their fantasies,
Especially unhealthy ones. The song
Began by making reference to the sea,
Because the sea is like a need so great
And deep it never can be swallowed. Then
The song explores some common myths
About the Cuban people and their folklore:
The story of a little Carib boy
Mistakenly abandoned to the sea;
The legend of a bird who wanted song
So desperately he gave up flight; a queen
Whose strength was greater than a rival king's.
The song goes on about morality,
And then there is a line about the sea,
How deep it is, how many creatures need
Its nourishment, how beautiful it is
To need. The song is ending now, because
I cannot bear to hear it any longer.
I call this song of needful love my voice.

El Día de los Muertos

In Mexico, I met myself one day
along the side of someone's private road.
I recognized the longing in my face,
I felt the heavy burden of the load
I carried. Mexico, I thought, was strange
and very dry. The private road belonged
to friends more powerful than I, enraged
but noble people who like me sang songs
in honor of the dead. In Mexico,
tradition is as heavy as the sun.
I stared into my eyes. Some years ago,
I told myself, I met a handsome man
who thought that I was Mexican. The weight
of some enormous pain, unspeakable
yet plain, was in his eyes; his shirt was white,
so white it blinded me. After it all
became more clear, and we were making love
beneath the cool sheet of the moon, I knew
we were alive. The tiny stars above
seemed strange and very far. A dry wind blew.
I gave myself to him, and then I asked
respectfully if I might touch his face.
I did not want to die. His love unmasked,
I saw that I had slept not with disgrace
but with desire. Along the desert road,
a cactus bloomed. As water filled my eyes,
I sang a song in honor of the dead.
They came for me. My grief was like a vise,
and in my blood I felt the virus teem.
My noble friends abandoned me beside

FROM *Diva*

(DUKE UNIVERSITY PRESS, 2000)

The Pelvic Exam

The speculum is silvery and cold.
The uterus has secrets to be told.
Abnormal bleeding after periods:

Blighted pregnancy, or cancer taking hold,
Infection, trauma silently withstood.
My speculum is silvery and cold,

Its jaws are open to the source of blood.
It enters her. Vaginal walls unfold.
"Abnormal bleeding after periods—"

I stop myself. "You're seventeen years old?"
She shivers as my fingers poke and prod.
My speculum is silvery and cold;

I look away from it to see her nod.
At first, the tears that drop are half-controlled.
Abnormal bleeding after periods

Has made her pain's unwilling centerfold,
The child I would safeguard if I could.
The speculum is silvery and cold,

The brute examination it allowed
Not consolation, more a wordless scold.
Abnormal bleeding after periods

Can only be so many things. Withheld
Until she knows, her sobs become a flood.
The speculum is silvery and cold

Upon the table where it sits, the blood
Now dried. This case, before you ask, is closed:
Abnormal bleeding after periods.
The speculum is silvery and cold.

The Gift of AIDS

I saw you coming toward me with a gift.
You wore the slippers made of Kaposi's,
The gown of night and soaking sweats. You moved
As if you had been photographed—you blurred
The trees you passed before. You held the box
Inside your chest somehow, the ribbons were
Your arteries, its corners were your spine
And ribs. I pleaded with you, pleaded that
You give me what you hid from me; you laughed
Like it was not as painful as it was for you,
And suddenly the ground was silver clouds
And we were so in love it was impossible
That you were dead. I saw you coming close,
I saw you and you had a gift for me,
The gift of AIDS and blood that was your heart,
Your beating heart, your beating, beating heart.

The Abdominal Exam

Before the glimmer of his sunken eyes,
What question could I answer with my lies?

Digesting everything, it's all so plain
In him, his abdomen so thin the pain

Is almost visible. I probe the lump
His boyfriend noticed first, my left hand limp

Beneath the pressure of the right. With AIDS,
You have to think lymphoma—swollen nodes,

A tender spleen, the liver's jutting edge—
It strikes me suddenly I will oblige

This hunger that announces death is near,
And as I touch him, cool and cavalier,

The language of beneath the diaphragm
Has told me where it's coming from

And where I'm going, too: soft skin to rocks,
The body reveling until it wrecks

Against the same internal, hidden shoal,
The treasures we can't hide, our swallowed gold.

from The Changing Face of AIDS

V. ELEGY FOR THE AIDS VIRUS

How difficult it is to say goodbye
to scourge. For years we were obsessed with you,
your complex glycoproteins and your sly,
haphazard reproduction, your restraint
in your resistance, how you bathed so slight
yet fierce in our most intimate secretions.
We will remember you for generations;
electron micrographs of you seem quaint
already, in the moment of our victory.
How difficult it is to claim one's right
to living honestly. The honesty
you taught was nothing quite as true

as death, but neither was it final. Yes,
we vanquished you, with latex, protease
inhibitors, a little common sense—
what's that, you say? That some remain at risk?
How dare you try to threaten us again!
Of course, you'd like to make outrageous claims
that some behaviors haven't changed, that some
have not had access to the drugs that mask
your presence in the body. Difficult
it is, how very sad, to see you strain
(no pun intended) at response—our quilts,
our bravest poetry, our deaths with grace

and dignity have put you in your place.
This elegy itself renounces you,
as from this consciousness you've been erased.

The love for you was very strong, the hot
pursuits so many of us reveled in—
but what once felt like love was really not.
I hardly know what I will find to hate
as much as I have loved and hated what
you brought to bear upon my verse, the weight
of your oppression and the joys of truth.
How difficult it is—to face the white
of nothingness, of clarity. We win!

X. REFINISHING THE HARDWOOD FLOORS

The day he came to give his estimate,
the rap he played came echoing amidst
the tall Victorians that line our street—
a jarring rumble, even in the cave
that they create. He wore a rumpled shirt
emblazoned with his name. "I'm Rafael—
it's nice to meet you, Dex." My hand seemed small
on shaking his, whose palm was etched and carved
with lines—it felt like corrugated steel.
We knew that he was ill; to do our part,
we try to offer jobs through special deals
for those in the community with AIDS.

He paused as we ascended, out of breath.
I wondered whether he was up to it:
our loft is huge, and traps the heat beneath
the skylights we put in last year. Besides—
the flecks of sawdust on the skeletal
black arms that braced him on the banister
were mixed with track marks, tiny dots of scars
along his veins. A loud dog barked outside,
which cued us to resume our climb. What changed,

so that I saw him shuffle down the hall,
delivered at its end to the airy stage,
cathedral-ceilinged, window panes so great

that in their frame his slender silhouette
seemed insignificant? He jotted down
some notes, unnerving me the longer that
he stayed. The room was getting hot, transformed
from what was heavenly beside the man
I loved (I felt the rush of it anew,
the thrill of making household plans with you),
to an approaching hell with Dex. His firm
touch interrupted me just then: inscribed
in shaky handwriting were figures penned
with, evident in their completeness, pride.
He told me he could start next week. At dawn

on the appointed day, he came with two
assistants. k.d. lang or Europop—
I wondered which cd would better do
to drown their racket out. Too frequently,
perhaps, I checked on them, my concentration
shot even worse by a recurrent thought:
a stranger in the house you and I bought.
The sanding led to toxic fumes; for three
long days we aired our new room's shiny floor
impatient to set foot in our creation.
I paid in cash, then rushed Dex out the door;
I felt so clean I cried, and couldn't stop.

A Death Perplexing

And when you died, it was perplexing. Songs
Reversed so that they were no longer songs;
The death of you was so perplexing, none
But I could see that you were really gone.
You lived so quietly that near the end
I hardly recognized you as my friend.
Instead, you were my lover, bodiless
And yet a hungry lover nonetheless.
You feasted on my heart, and I on yours;
Your eyes were just the first this death of yours
Consumed, as soon you tasted mine. A death
Perplexing as the death of you—your death,
Not mine, your death the death it took some time
To see completely. At a loss, untamed,
My grief bears no explaining—I am dead,
A death perplexing as the life I lead.

My Reasoning

Illogical, yet not illogical,
The world proceeds in fits toward its destruction.
The world is ready for it. At luncheons,
In killing fields, the unbelievable

Is happening: poached eggs, crushed children's skulls.
It isn't hard, it isn't criminal.
The world proceeds with what is possible.
You say you love me; sunlight seems a skill

That anyone could learn, so sensible,
So clear. We walk across a fallow field,
Wondering what we know, what we can feel.
You say the world is what's invisible,

As if the wind that clasps my throat were real,
As if anyone deserves miracles.
The world goes on, both indestructible
And so terribly, terribly fragile

I'm almost too afraid to step again.
You say you love me, like that's logical,
And stoop to pick a buttercup, so small
I could have crushed it, tiny yellow sun;

I know that something's happening to me—
That in this world, some things aren't possible.
I look at you and see you're very ill.
You dart away. The world moves, quietly.

Recognition

That night, while he was beaten, I was stretched
in sleep beside the man I love. I'd dreamed
like anybody does; my heart half-leapt
when I awoke to singing in the shower.
The semi-darkness promised to grow true;

it seemed that life was good, your voice like grace.
As unaware as I was, you were happy.
We fixed our breakfast as we always do.
I toasted bread, too mindful of the hour,
our dog beneath me thinking she's a puppy,

pushing her nose against me, begging treats.
While tears washed blood in streaks from off his face
before the muted dawn, I watched you grind
our coffee, spilling some like dirt across
the green Formica countertop. It felt

like joy, to watch your squint-eyed measuring—
two cups, not more, of glinting water in
the clear glass pot. The simple ritual
that marries light and liquid, elements
that somehow join us—then, you smiled, as if

to prove us safe, or that the trees outside
could recognize us. Somewhere else, the boy
lost hope. A bit annoyed, I wiped the grounds
you always leave behind; by then, they'd found
what first was taken for an animal

that hunters lashed against a barbed-wire fence.
We drove together to the hospital

and held each other's hands, as usual,
bracing ourselves for others' misery,
or maybe nothing in particular,

or something else we'd yet to learn to see.
The boy was dying, rushed by ambulance
across a stretch of frozen countryside.
You kissed me sneakily on going up,
our elevator empty but for us;

your love, I felt, was rising into me.
But later, when we learned with disbelief
how Matthew Shepard died from injuries
he suffered as a consequence of this
same love, I wondered whether I deserved

to die that way, incomprehensibly
as why you couldn't hold me while you cried;
I wondered whether he had touched us as
he left an unfamiliar world, and whether
what he found was anything like grace.

The Mental Status Exam

What is the color of the mind? Beneath
The cranium it's pinkish gray, with flecks
Of white mixed in. What is the mind's motif?
Depends on what you mean: it's either sex
Or it's a box, release or pessimism.
Remember these three things: ball, sorrow, red.
Count backward, from one-hundred down by sevens.
What is the color of the mind? It's said
That love can conquer all—interpret, please.
And who's the president? What year is it?
The mind is timeless, dizzy, unscrupulous;
The mind is sometimes only dimly lit.
Just two more silly questions: Can you sing
For us? Do you remember those three things?

Last Rites

Exhaustion enters me, as winter does
The emptiness of January days:
With clarity. These trees, starved down to bones,
Seem barely able to withstand the weight
Of what I am resigned to call the truth.

Last night I watched it happen. It was death,
As usual and present as the view
Of downtown Boston from my patient's room.
Before the bleed, he pointed out for me
A wisp of smoke that rose like mystery

Against the certain, dusk-blue sky. "I pray,"
He whispered to me as I probed his liver,
My hands, as in I pressed, brought close together.
Outside, a siren dwindled to a sigh.
"Do you believe in Christ?" I tried to pry

The image of the smoke (which wasn't more
Than some exhaust from an anonymous
Brick chimney) from my dimming faith that was
At once incomprehensible as stars
And as unknowable as they were far,

Appearing just above the skyscrapers.
I watched them from beside his bed, the world
And all its lights less glorious somehow;
I wondered, heartlessly, at who we were.
I didn't pray—I had forgotten how—

And then it came. The torrent of his blood,
Unstanchable, in roaring waves so full

I was less horrified than plain amazed.
His life flared out in red before my eyes;
The clots that lingered in his mouth were slick

As cherry candies on his startled tongue.
He looked at me, as pale as I was dumb,
And faded to his final peace. With God?
I searched the skyline for his wisp of smoke,
But night had rendered it invisible.

FROM *Landscape with Human Figure*

(DUKE UNIVERSITY PRESS, 2002)

The Couple

Releasing his determined grip, he lets
her take the spoon; the cube of cherry Jell-O
teeters on it, about to drop as if
no precipice were any steeper, no

oblivion more final. Earlier
today, he hemorrhaged, the blood so fast
a torrent that it splattered onto her.
She washed herself, unwillingly it seemed,

perhaps not wanting to remove what was
his ending life from where it stained her skin.
I watch them now, the way they love across
the gap between them that their bodies make:

how cruel our lifelong separation seems.
The ward keeps narrowing itself to that
bright point outside his door — the muffled screams
along a hallway to the absolute —

and as I turn away from them it's not
their privacy, or even my beginning shame
I wish I could escape. It is the light,
the awful light of what we know must come.

On Christmas Eve

One year you gave me lavish jewelry,
which I mistook for lasting love.

One year you gave me guileless poetry
which I believed was not enough.

One year you gave me an infection,
and I was glad you were alive.

This year, I give you your reflection.
Look at me, and know my grief.

Next year, we'll give no gifts at all.
You knew I loved you. Night falls.

The Four Humours

I. BLOOD

We wondered if the rumors got to her.
I'd seen her with that other girl behind
the Stop and Shop when I was walking home
from school one day. I swear, the two of them
were kissing, plain as that, the grass so high
it brushed their cheeks. I told my teacher so,
and maybe it was her who called their folks.
Before too long, it was like everyone
in town had heard. We waited for them at
the dime store once, where Cedric grabbed her tits
and said *I'll learn you how to love how God
intended it, you ugly fucking dyke.*
Thing was, she wasn't ugly like you'd think.
She had a certain quality, a shyness
maybe, and I'd describe the way she laughed
as kind of gentle. Anyway, we never saw her with
that girl again. They say she got depressed—
shit, at the service all of us got tearful.
I got to thinking what an awful sight
it was, all that red blood—it wasn't in
the papers, but I heard Melissa's mother,
who was the nurse in the Emergency
that night, say how she was just covered up
in blood. I can't think how you bring yourself
to cut your throat like that yourself—I asked
the counselor they called in to the school,
and she said something like, *What better ink
to write the language of the heart?* I guess

it proves that stuff from Bible school they say,
that such a life of sin breeds misery.

II. PHLEGM

"My brain is draining from my head,"
he said as once again he blew
his nose. The clock read 3 AM;

its second hand swept slowly through
another viscous minute. Dead
to even nurses sticking them

for new IVs, the other ones
slept off their benders soundlessly.
"I'm losing my intelligence,"

he said, and blew. My patience waned.
He thought he was the president:
Dementia, KS, HIV

were printed in his problem list.
"And plus, I'm getting feverish."
I can't recall his name, but I

remember hating him—grim wish
that he would hurry up and die.
Just then, he took my hand, and kissed

the back of it as though I were
a princess in his foreign land.
"My lady, you are beautiful,"

he said, and coughed again. Unsure
of what to say, my own throat burned.
He said, "You can't know what I feel."

III. BILE

A gun went off and killed a little girl
the day my friend was diagnosed with cancer.
I walked through Central Park; a black dog snarled
at squirrels chattering like they had answers.

The day my friend was diagnosed with cancer
I dreamed of killing someone with a knife.
The squirrels, chattering, had easy answers
to all my angry questions about life—

a homeboy threatened someone with a knife
not far from where a cop showed off his gun,
an angry answer to most questions about life.
I watched the squirrels hop, the yuppies run;

the cop approached the black kids with his gun.
I wondered how much longer she would live;
the squirrels scattered when the homeboy ran.
I wondered if she'd ever been in love,

I wondered who would pray for her to live,
forgive her for her anger and her weaknesses.
I wondered why it hurt to fall in love.
The cop tried aiming past me, toward the woods.

Forgive us for our anger, for our weaknesses:
Through Central Park, past the black dog's snarls,
the cop gave chase. A skirmish in the woods—
the gun went off. *No!* shrieked a little girl.

IV. MELANCHOLY

We picked at it with sticks at first, until
an older kid named Samuel arrived.

He dropped a heavy rock right on its skull;
we watched as thick black slime began to ooze
from somewhere just below its heart, or where
we thought its heart should be. "Raccoon,"
said someone solemnly. The landscaper—
sweat gleaming, like the polished figurines
my mother wouldn't ever let me touch—
regarded us with keen suspicion from
across the street. We learned what it could teach;
like any body's secrets, the sublime
receded toward the fact of death. I knew
both sadness, and disgust in love's untruths.

from Afraid of the Dark

A black man in the ER waits for me.
I take my time, because the sign-out says
he's homeless, alcoholic, probably
a shooter too, complaining of three days
of headache. Fever, not quite 102.
A cough, and short of breath. It's either AIDS
or just another boring case of flu—
a list of other diagnoses fades
as I catch sight of him, half hidden by
the puke-stained, yellow curtain. "He looks fine,"
my intern gripes. A disembodied cry
suggests the possibility of pain—
I notice all the doctors here are white,
while nearly all the patients that we treat

are black, or brown. He stares back, wearily,
as though he knows the next experiment
in which he's made the subject has to be
as flawed as all the others. Once we've spent
a couple minutes on his history—
we'll fill the gaps ourselves—it's time to find
a vein. The Great Society,
Tuskegee, Martin Luther King—though blind,
my stick surprises me with how his blood
so briskly flows, as if by force of habit.
My intern asks me whether we'll exclude
immunocompromise—"I bet he has it,"
she crows—but I am thinking of his eyes,
the blankness of a hope not realized.

What I Would Give

What I would like to give them for a change
is not the usual prescription with
its hubris of the power to restore,
to cure; what I would like to give them, ill
from not enough of lying in the sun
not caring what the onlookers might think
while feeding some banana to their dogs—
what I would like to offer them is this,
not reassurance that their lungs sound fine,
or that the mole they've noticed change is not
a melanoma, but instead of fear
transfigured by some doctorly advice
I'd like to give them my astonishment
at sudden rainfall like the whole world weeping,
and how ridiculously gently it
slicked down my hair; I'd like to give them that,
or the joy I felt while staring in your eyes
as you learned epidemiology
(the science of disease in populations),
the night around our bed like timelessness,
like comfort, like what I would give to them.

FROM *The Enemy*

(DUKE UNIVERSITY PRESS, 2007)

from Eighteen Days in France

WHY WE NEVER TRAVEL

I've always wanted to return. Before
I learned the body's caves and slums,
I knew a sacred world my lover claims
lay not so far from here. It wasn't fear
that kept me—maybe it was something in
the river's murmuring, the sunset's peace
that did. The wounds of men are imprecise,
but even so, can kill. Inside their skin
I wandered, long vacations in their lungs,
my souvenirs a vertebra or tooth.
I lost my lover on a mountain path
above a waterfall that carved with song
its granite bed. I've always wanted to
go back, that bloodless peak, no heart as true.

MARILYN IN PARIS

Below the Place de la Sorbonne, we heard
them playing—bluesy jazz from a duet—
an old piano, and a clarinet.
A woman, housed in something like a shroud
of plastic bags, looked on with sadness,
and joy—the paradox is understood
in Paris, capital of the unfairly good.
It's later, when we wander along side-streets,
hands clasped for just a moment, that I wonder
exactly how that bruised piano landed there,
cramped sidewalk of a busy thoroughfare,
and why its tender music seemed an answer

to questions more keen. In her studio,
the master writes her poems: She would know.

MAKING SENSE OF THE CURRENCY IN LINE FOR LE MUSÉE PICASSO

However closer it might seem to art—
the brightly colored bills, the graceful figures
about to waltz off heavy coins—it pays for
the gasoline, the decaf and baguette.
To use a public toilet costs two francs,
a little less than what I give the man
without a leg whose sign I understand
(another universal language, inked
in French, called poverty and suffering)—
the smell of money, like the smell of piss,
is recognizable in any place.
For thirty francs, we're in: like broken things
too priceless to be thrown away, we see
Picassos everywhere, stark misery.

TACHYCARDIA AT THE CATHEDRAL OF NOTRE DAME

I'm here, but think of them, the ones I've left
for colleagues to console about the test
that's positive, the virus we detect
despite the triple cocktail, the shift
in white count signaling another—what?
I'm here, but think pneumonia, GC,
lymphoma, specters that will not recede
as easily as we re-think, forget—
I'm here, another country where I wish
there were no AIDS, and they are here with me,
my patients and my friends, their poetry

as yet unwritten, brows not feverish,
still here, with me, where I administer
just joy—pulses loudly beating, hearts stirred.

THE UNNAMED UNDERSTOOD

All day, we searched for it, the restaurant
that Marilyn had claimed served only boar.
We didn't know what we were looking for
as through each sun-worn village we would squint
at homely storefronts with their tilted signs
that usually announced "FERMÉ." A taste
for game (intensified by all the craze
about "mad cow"—though each we passed seemed sane,
bovinely calm, behind its barbed-wire fence)
had led to our obsessed pursuit. We found
a likely candidate, but like its town,
it was completely boarded up—in French,
spray-painted reasons we could not decipher,
as if tattooed on it, names of dead lovers.

DETOUR

Why is it that this verdant countryside
reminds me of their bodies? Muscular
like Gary, or Tyrell, the way they were—
in almost casual repose, pre-AIDS.
We're getting lost among the vineyards now,
impressed by the occasional chateau,
each one a grandiose yet heartfelt vow
against surrender. Why did I not know
enough to save them? Birds fly low, as if
reluctant to be parted from forbidden
earthly consorts; the entire world seems hidden,

for just a moment, by some passing wisps
of cloud. The stolen sun, returned to us,
is harrowing as it is glorious.

POSTCARD FROM BURGUNDY

Dear Marilyn,
                We've made it to Bouilland!
There's almost nothing here—we hiked last night
along a hillside road which at its height
was crowned with firs and poplars joined in stands,
last pilgrims to a solemn, ruined abbey.
I thought of you as we ascended, breath
as urgent as the hunger of your grief.
Above the broken transept's arches, happy
birds dipped and soared. The moon was rising fast,
to cast its eeriness around the place;
the columbines beneath the Queen Anne's lace
seemed each a tragicomic jester's face
that jeered but pitied us on our return,
taught something I'm not sure is ever learned.

SUMMER VACATION READING

Leaving the inn, we step out into sun
so bright I flash back to the white ER:
surrounding vineyards neat as cornrowed hair,
exposed earth black as her deflated skin.
I almost yearn for that lost urgency,
when briefly doctors treated love as a scourge,
French novels giving way to French research,
sad Madame Bovary to HIV.
When I touched her bony arm, it was not
impossible that she would die. In fact,

she did, blood poisoned by our bumbling acts
as much as by what seemed the opposite
of this complacency. Her silent stare
still burns as she refuses our best care.

HOSPICES DE BEAUNE, HÔTEL-DIEU

How little we've advanced in medicine:
beneath the fifteenth-century stained glass
their gruesome transphrenations let release
the noxious humours they thought caused by sin
as much as by disease. The images
and instruments that they preserved recall
our human needs, for doing good as well
as punishing the awful godlessness
that agony is sometimes taken for.
Saint Michael weighed their souls, his placid face
of little comfort as they died; Christ's grace
remains elusive, as so many more
of us are damned than saved. The sisters prayed,
as I do, now—mistrustful, still afraid.

THE OLIVE GROVE

How many centuries ago these trees
were planted is unknown, but some have guessed
the Romans planned these hilltop terraces.
The scowling faces in the bark agree
on nothing in their silent arguments,
except that they'll bear fruit again, green globes
hard with their bitterness. The sunset glows
and sends long shadows stretching through their midst,
akin to how I yearn for you—how old
is need, how tangled up in ancient knots.

You've wandered off from me, drawn by the scents
of lavender and jasmine on the cold
breeze rising up from where a garden pleads:
the olive grove's grudged shelter seems betrayed.

ROMAN FRÉJUS

Decaying columns overgrown with weeds
are all that's really here, the skeleton
of some vast beast left bleaching in the sun
that makes us wonder how it died. Faint words
in Latin dedicate a toppled arch;
small bits of colored rock in a mosaic
depict a noblewoman's painted, stoic,
compliant lips. Too easily, we search
for something we might reconstruct as us:
Did two men ever walk what seems to be
a road beside the baths as quietly
as we do now, in love? Ridiculous—
and yet to know that neither will we last
is why we've come, enamored of the past.

POSTCARD FROM MONACO

Dear M.,
        We're here, where countries' borders seem
so trivial. We simply drove right in,
no passports necessary, no long line
to have your suitcase searched. It's like a dream,
this kind of freedom, even if it does
seemed purchased by the filthy rich. Rolls Royce,
Ferrari, Porsche—is luxury the price
one has to pay to live in paradise?
(The gated villas make the cars look cheap.)

I've wondered what it's possible to own—
right now, I'd give it all away to know
J.'s joy as he picks his way down the beach
to steal a dip in this ownerless sea.
We send our love—he is in to his knees!

FOUND AMONG DISCARDED PHOTOGRAPHS

We were there, however briefly. What changed?
The place itself cannot remember us—
the blackbirds that seemed caged inside the ribs
of pines dispersed upon the church bell's clang.
But we were there, remarking on the beauty of
the town's small square, the anonymity
of shops and restaurants, and balconies
whose red bougainvillea flung themselves off
ruined by unrequited love. We've changed
since we were there, and what we can recall—
the injury of red blooms on white walls,
the unfelt emptying of startled wings—
is nothing but God's punishment for all
we have forgotten in ourselves to praise,
for all such wonders truth could not reprise.

REST STOP NEAR THE ITALIAN BORDER

Alps crowding in the distance, gas tank low,
we stop beneath the diesel clouds of trucks—
black radiators, ugly stars of bugs
squashed flat. You say you need to go.
A Muslim family, Algerian
perhaps, drifts by, the woman's robes
bright fluttering amidst the roar the road's
unending traffic raises. Evian,

some candy to defuse my garlic breath—
you're off, determined, and so I'm left
with just the warmth of your hand's soft,
negligible weight. A hand I held, near death,
back home—I can't recall his name,
but speeding, inescapable, was what came.

POSTCARD MAILED FROM THE AIRPORT

Dear M.,
        I'm writing now from CDG.
It seems impossible we're going home—
so much we haven't seen. Next year, to Rome?
By then, all this will be a memory.
And yet, I know it's changed me, being here
on this old earth. They're here, you know, my patients,
the ones who died on me too young—their passions,
their laughter and first tastes of caviar,
their spindly arms that reach out toward the sun
amidst the plane trees and the monuments.
They talked to me from deep in catacombs;
they smelled like grass, in parks rinsed clean by rain.
So many parks in Paris—in warm bread
broken, their steaming breath—last mornings, shared.

You Bring Out the Doctor in Me

after Sandra Cisneros

You bring out the doctor in me
The smart perfume of antiseptics
The possibly unsound heart through the stethoscope
The naked under this paper drape in me.

You bring out the this won't hurt a bit in me
The scrubs that look like pajamas
The crude anatomical diagrams
The skin is the largest organ in me.

I'd let you draw my blood
The sting of my own needles,
The cold metal of fact in me.
Test it for secret love, for HIV.
I'd die for you, to have you in me.
Just you. No latex.
Just you and me.

You bring out the health care proxy in me.
Do not resuscitate,
Do not intubate me.
You bring out the chaplain praying in me.
The IV bag hanging, glassy fluids in me.
The nurse in white sneakers toileting me.
The morphine drip, the dream of you dreaming me.
Maybe I'm dying. Maybe.

You bring out the helplessness in me
The limits of knowledge in me
The inability to cry in me.

You bring out the doctor in me.
You can't cure me: adore me.
Let me show you. Love
The only way I know how.

Tuesday Morning

The world awakening again, great stretch
of sky, its limbs the pinkish cirrus clouds
that lift away. But how to bless the day
already crowded with the sounds of trucks
downshifting, laden with their cargo, blare

of morning headlines while my love works out,
the neighbors' barking mutts. It's all been said
before, and even the embarrassment
of my erection makes no novel point:
What need is there for pleasure, when today

I'll diagnose a man with cancer, not
know what to say. Believing in the poem
provides not much relief. I hear the grief
in a descending airplane's roar, arrived
from Buenos Aires or from Amsterdam—

the clouds embrace the disappearing moon,
but even this transparent metaphor
offers little comfort. No poet cares
for such deceptions anymore, and words
don't cure. The sky continues brightening

but irony is lost on me forever.
Who wants religion, who would ask forgiveness?
Car door slams; momentary angled light
sweeps through my half-dark bedroom like the flight
of some enormous, awkward bird. I see

some brief connection, maybe. Some small joy,
stupid as sleep, yet perfect as the dream
one never can remember. Getting up,
I tangle with my bathrobe—slippers fit—
and mumble to myself the morning's prayer.

Arriving

We're newcomers to an old place. The house
was built in 1860 (so we think);
since then, the Portuguese fishermen
and the faded, artsy bohemians
have come and started now to go, replaced
by "guppies" driving Lexuses. Our street
is lined with lindens, home to chickadees
that play in the elaborate display
of whirligigs, birdbaths, wind chimes, and what's
got to be the world's most complex bird feeder
constructed by the man who lived next door
year-round, until at eighty-eight he died
of what the rumors say was "just pneumonia."
Being doctors, we are privy to much more
than other weekenders with second homes:
we know about the prostate three doors down;
across the street, it's diabetic feet
and cataracts. Some friends who've seen our place
have asked us when another like it might
become available; we sipped our drinks
beneath the twilit sky, approving of
the light, the certain quality it has
that no one could articulate. Ice clinked
as if in harmony with the cascade
of notes from those wind chimes next door; I knew
the realtors had been there yesterday.
Another neighbor down the street has AIDS,
as if to prove us not so different—
"They told me I could live with it," he'd said,
"for twenty years—and now I get lymphoma,"

while well-fed birds bounced from above like balls
belonging to the gods' unruly children.
Arriving here, perhaps like us he thought
he might escape; perhaps he sought the light
the artists and the Portuguese came here
to venerate each in their human way.
Expatriates like them, I want to say . . .
A painting we admired on a cold day,
off-season, on Commercial Street: two men
working nets in a small boat, churning sea,
the light between them captured perfectly,
belonging, it would seem, to everyone.
We left the gallery and headed home.

Absolution

The moon rises over the willow tree.
It looks like an aspirin in the sky,
bright white pill for all the world's ailments. I
remember Nonna at age eighty-three

refusing to take all her medicine.
She said she'd rather be read to in bed,
an old-fashioned love story, or instead
an article from *Reader's Digest*. When

my uncle found her one morning, her face
in halves, one peaceful and the other slack,
the doctor said she'd had a major stroke.
Two white pills sat there on a china plate,

just like the ones you bring me now. The night
is like this headache I can't shake, so full
of shapeless troubles: brave young soldiers killed,
the rising price of crude, gay marriage rights,

and worst of all, my fear of losing you.
"Doctors make the worst patients," you declare,
which sounds like something she would say before
she lost her words. Like her, I want a few

good moments rooting for my hero to
return, I want a happy ending. "No,"
I say, and push the pills away. You go,
the moon outside our window bathing you

in what seems, briefly, the absence of pain.

On Doctoring

for Thomas L. Delbanco, MD

A day like any other: 8 AM
and I am listening to him explain

exactly where the pain is—that it hurts
to bend the knee, especially the part

beneath the scar from where the surgeon scraped
out all the cartilage. A paper drape

provides its square of modesty (or tries
to, anyway; his boxer shorts have stripes,

blue ones, I notice half-distractedly)—
I move the joint for him, a gentle sweep

through its full range of motion. Marvelous,
the body's workmanship, how perfect is

its service to the soul it shelters, each
soft hair along the shin enshrining touch,

this way we're made to need another's care.
An awkward shifting, a throat is cleared—

enough, to realize this truth. I draw
the curtain with a screech, and glimpse the dawn

give over to the day. Like any other,
my patient gives the gift of how we suffer.

Sick Day

The clinking of recyclables picked up
accompanies an unheard benediction.
The magnetism of new passengers
pulls the heavy bus from traffic; God, how
particularly orange is this glass
of juice, so sweet it teaches us salvation.
Bell tower of a church, O pinnacle
beneath which she fed pigeons yesterday,
continue your protection of the weak,
uphold the sky, make her in her black shawl
like Grandmother's seem beautiful to me
again. We all get sick and die, we all
remember something as it happened once,
the way the houses' roofs across the street
can seem like books are closing slowly on
the stories of those inside. Holy, holy,
holy Lord, it is February, weeks
from when the sun will blaze like Florida,
hours before *Angels in America*
comes on again. What is left to be said,
the distant war like humankind's first holler
in the desert—do not leave us alone!—
when all we have are these imperfect bodies?
Feed a fever, starve a cold: still, we hunger,
so we pray with our sore throats *Grant us peace.*

FROM *Alternative Medicine*

(DUKE UNIVERSITY PRESS, 2013)

Calendar

I threw out 1998 today.
What had I hoped for then, what days were marked?
My grandfather was dead that year, by March.
We mourned him in the cemetery's gray,

wishing we had some lost time with him back.
"You can't hold on to memories," he'd say,
his lungs half-gone, his heart long since betrayed.
He kept a yellowing almanac

on some shelves near his bed. Some fishing lures,
and toy soldiers and photographs—bright days
that he somehow kept on living, the phase
of the black moon each week less of a cure.

Best planting days, lost anniversaries—
what do we know? Thrown open in the trash
those since-forgotten months, the perfect halves
of equinox, the year's early first freeze.

The Common Mental Health Disorders of Immigrants

I. POST-TRAUMATIC STRESS DISORDER

My nephew watches the survivalist
on television drink his own dark piss,
eat spiders, clamber down a waterfall—
he's white and blue-eyed, good-looking, agile.
He makes a shelter from his parachute.
Behind him, no one chases after him,
besides the desert's looming black eagle
as silent as a shadow, bored as God.
He doesn't hope to have a better life.
His thirst is momentary, hunger an
imagined state; his sister doesn't sell
herself to British tourists so her kids
can have school books. Dogs barking distantly,
flashlight beams needling the night, nowhere
to go but in the steps of those before.
That night, they ate cold beans from cans; they drank
the water pooled inside a cast-off tire.
They left the little girl with diarrhea
asleep beneath a rocky ledge. No one
found a parachute to make a tent, or
drank his own piss in order to survive.

II. DEPRESSION

She smokes, as if she could inhale it all
and make it vanish: all the poisonous
miasmas, all the mysterious dreams,
the tears my grandfather shed, where she hid
while soldiers smashed the grand piano, black

as a deep lake, to pieces. Now, her house
is small and spare: telenovelas blare,
though the volume's turned off, in black-and-white
from a room's corner, ashtrays filling with
what her lungs cannot, in the end, absorb.
Her eyes are bleary, sunk in, with dark rings,
tender from life's beating. Did such a place
exist? I imagine huge banyan trees
encircling the nearby swamp, their ropes
dragging the whole world down into jungle;
screams of parrots at dusk, and the knowledge
that when they were quieted, danger lurked;
the hopelessness of learning Beethoven
in a small Cuban town, her father's cigarette
decomposing to cinder while she played.
There was a patio; a fountain tinkled.
She has his eyes, dark and handsome and beaten.
Miami's highways purr outside somewhere,
like unseen predators hunting the dark.
As she smokes, the TV making its ghosts
dance on her linoleum floor, I see
again the resemblance. I see her breathe,
inhaling memories, becoming him.
Now, almost quiet, it is almost safe.

III. ANXIETY

It's 1969. I'm five. The man
is knocking. Green shag carpet like a lawn
of chemicals. My mother vacuums it.
I fear the television's cloudy eye.
The man is knocking at our door. Outside,
it's winter in New Jersey, confusing

what's dry, what's cold: the salt-stained street looks parched,
my mother's face looks sunburned. The man knocks;
he has a black briefcase, looks official.
She mutters to herself, like we're in church.
Outside, the winter day seems tilted in the small
suburban windows of our house, a "ranch"
that lacks the cattle and the horses of
my father's fabled Cuban past. He knocks.
My father combs his hair so carefully
it's like he's trying to tell me something.
The vacuum cleaner whines with righteous rage,
soft pings of detritus consumed oddly
satisfying. Meanwhile, the knocking stops.
My mother studies lampshades, curtains, me,
the vacuum cleaner whining at her feet.
She bites her lower lip, alone with us,
alone with winter's tilted, cold, dry days;
the kitchen sparkles with her loneliness,
as if being seen through a film of tears.
I realize I fear he won't come back,
that we can never return home again.

Heart Grow Fonder

for Eve

The leg bone's connected to the shin bone.
An apple a day keeps the doctor away.
A little voice inside me said, "Beware."

A tumor big as a grapefruit killed her.
Tamoxifen, oxycodone, Bengay.
The breastbone's connected to the rib bone.

Like a patient etherized, I can't say
what evening looks like, but I feel alone.
A little voice inside me said, "Unfair."

"My brain's a sieve," she'd say. We mourned her hair.
She'd get lost on the way to San Jose.
The rib bone's connected to the back bone.

I plunged my heart in San Francisco Bay.
A scar across her chest: one breast was gone.
A little voice inside me said, "I'm scared."

Some final pleasures: slices of ripe pear,
massages strangely not unlike foreplay.
The back bone's connected to the neck bone.

Old voicemails from her that I still replay.
"Physician, heal thyself," sweetly intones
the little voice inside me I can't bear.

We'd read together almost every day.
After great pain, a formal feeling comes—
the neck bone's connected to the head bone.
A little voice inside me says, "Beware."

The Reading

In a clearing bounded by Philosophy
and Self-Help, twenty folding chairs stood fast
in little lines lean as a poem. Most
were empty still, like possibilities
that might yet be considered. Patiently,
a few dignified older ladies sat,
and in the back, scowling, the requisite
unbalanced but still harmless refugee
of the city's more insensitive streets.
Pathetic, if not insignificant
it seemed, as the cash registers up front
scanned tell-alls of gay stars who once were straight
and novels coding what we're told we seek.
A pair of college students drifted in,
their composition notebooks and pale skin
blank, ready to be written on. None spoke
until one of the bored store managers
appeared and gave the introduction. Brief
applause. Then, just as she began to read,
you took my hand, to meet the universe.

Health

While jogging on the treadmill at the gym,
that exercise in getting nowhere fast,
I realized we need a health pandemic.
Obesity writ large no more, Alzheimer's
forgotten, we could live carefree again.
We'd chant the painted shaman's sweaty oaths,
we'd kiss the awful relics of the saints,
we'd sip the bitter tea from twisted roots,
we'd listen to our grandmothers' advice.
We'd understand the moonlight's whispering.
We'd exercise by making love outside,
and afterward, while thinking only of
how much we'd lived in just one moment's time,
forgive ourselves for wanting something more:
to praise the memory of long-lost need,
or not to live forever in a world
made painless by our incurable joy.

Hospital Song

Someone is dying alone in the night.
The hospital hums like a consciousness.
I see their faces where others see blight.

The doctors make their rounds like satellites,
impossible to fathom distances.
Someone is dying alone under lights,

deficient in some electrolyte.
A mother gives birth: life replenishes.
I see pain in her face where others see fright.

A woman with breast cancer seems to be right
when she refuses our assurances
that we won't let her die alone tonight;

I see her face when I imagine flight,
when I dream of respite. Life punishes
us, faces searching ours for that lost light

which we cannot restore, try as we might.
The nurses' white sneakers say penances,
contrite as someone dying in the night.

As quiet as mercy, the morning's rites
begin. Over an old man's grievances,
his face contorted in the early light,

an aide serenely tends to him, her slight
black figure fleeting, yet all hopefulness—
her face the face of others who see light,
like someone dying at peace in the night.

Faith Healing

The tiny silver crucifix she wore
enacted what it seemed we did to her.

She rested in the bed, not at peace yet,
she said, but trying to forgive. The dead

moved quietly around the room, unseen:
last week, a man with liver cancer keened

where she did now, before he passed; and then
another woman whose lymphoma drenched

her in cold sweats, her lymph nodes thick and massed
wherever I had pressed. "Dear Lord," I said,

attempting what I thought was prayer, "—Lord,
forgive me for not healing them." Unsaid,

the words of her forgiveness came to me
like kindness, like a sudden memory.

The tiny crucifix refused to bleed;
instead, it shone there like a misplaced need,

a way to understand the blameless night.
Adjusting my ophthalmoscope's light,

I peered inside her, seeking what we may
of pain. I saw what she had tried to say:

the pulse of blood, the silence of my heart;
forgiveness, not impossible, but hard.

Iatrogenic

You say, "I do this to myself." Outside,
my other patients wait. Maybe snow falls;
we're all just waiting for our deaths to come,
we're all just hoping it won't hurt too much.
You say, "It makes it seem less lonely here."
I study them, as if the deep red cuts
were only wounds, as if they didn't hurt
so much. The way you hold your upturned arms,
the cuts seem aimed at your unshaven face.
Outside, my other patients wait their turns.
I run gloved fingertips along their course,
as if I could touch pain itself, as if
by touching pain I might alleviate
my own despair. You say, "It's snowing, Doc."
The snow, instead of howling, soundlessly
comes down. I think you think it's beautiful;
I say, "This isn't all about the snow,
is it?" The way you hold your upturned arms,
I think about embracing you, but don't.
I think, "We do this to ourselves." I think
the falling snow explains itself to us,
blinding, faceless, and so deeply wounding.

The Third Step in Obtaining an Arterial Blood Gas

First, gather your equipment: squares of gauze,
iodine swab, needle (23-gauge),
and don't forget the cup of ice you need
to send it to the lab. Next, find the pulse
(did I forget to mention sterile gloves?)
between your index and third fingers where
you need to make your stick. Press hard enough,
obliterating it for just a beat
or two, imagining the artery—
release the pressure gently as you bend
back the patient's wrist. See the artery
beneath the skin, and as you aim, don't think,
this part's the hardest part, don't think about
the pain, just focus on the flash of red
that means you're in. Then hold it steady as
the plunger moves invisibly, like God
or the force of your will is moving it—
the blood draws itself, pretty fucking cool,
huh? Just like magic, right—but it's really not.
Now practice one on that gorked CVA
we just admitted. She won't feel a thing.

For All the Freaks of the World

after Mary Campbell

A friend of mine once wrote a poem for Buttons,
then famous as the world's smallest horse.
I felt sorry for her, my friend I mean,
because all she could see was the irony,
the confinement of such a spectacle
in such a pitifully small stall.

Then there was Mister Pinky, the world's smallest dog:
five inches tall, dressed in a pink tux
complete with tiny bow tie
and a dapper pink fedora.
I was shocked to learn he's really a she.
I read about it in the newspaper.

I went to a conference once
and met a woman who was once a man.
She had severe liver failure, and wanted
to write a poem about her illness.
She said the hospital made her crazy.
I tried to help her. I'm not sure if I did.

I looked in the mirror this morning
and stared at my pitifully thinning hair.
When I was in college, a girl who liked me
but didn't know I was gay
said I looked like George Michael.
We remember the weirdest things.

There's a couple of well-nourished queers
whose wedding announcement
appears in the Sunday paper
complete with a picture of them
in their white tuxes and white bow ties
feeding each other huge mouthfuls of cake.

A friend of mine, who is a nearsighted poet,
tells me her girlfriend is leaving her.
She can't earn a decent living wage
teaching composition at MIT.
Someone should write a poem about
the billions her students will make cloning genes
and curing cancer, or liver failure.

I read in the newspaper once
about some poor sheep named Dolly
who was made to give birth to her own clone.
They looked alike. I thought it was ironic,
because who can tell the difference
between most sheep anyway?

When I was a student
at Harvard Medical School,
I worked in an immunology lab
that was run by a Holocaust survivor's son.
The research involved harvesting eyes
from genetically mutant, hairless mice.
I can't remember much else.

Once, I tried to help a homeless man in the street.
"I'm a doctor," I said.
His breath stank of vomit,
and one eye was white like glue.

His belly was swollen from liver failure.
He said I had hands like a woman's.

Sometimes I wish I could see Buttons
in her pitiful little stall.
After, I'd eat a corn dog and a fried Twinkie,
then climb a hill to be alone
with the wind in my remaining hair
to write a poem for all the freaks of the world.

Recent Past Events

It wasn't so miraculous back then.
Some said we had their blood on our prim hands.
We were ashamed of our good appetites.
We marched together in gay pride parades.
We feared their blood. We prayed for it to end.
We learned the names of lands in Africa:
Botswana, Ghana, Tanzania, Chad.
We adopted universal precautions.
We prayed for it to end. We feared their blood.
We were afraid to call our parents who
we knew would think the worst. We learned to speak
in acronyms. We watched two women kiss
on television late one night. We cried.
We handed out free condoms in the Fens.
Remember when it seemed miraculous
that most of our close friends weren't dead? We feared
their blood. We were ashamed. We went on trips
to Africa. We saw a leopard kill
an antelope, we saw the vast red dunes
Namibia is famous for. We cried
at patients' funerals. We handed out
clean needles in the Fens. We feared their blood.
We touched each other carefully at night,
remembered when it felt miraculous.
Remember when his cheekbones didn't jut
so much? We had their blood on our clean hands.
We were ashamed of living while they died.
We cooked for friends. We prayed for it to end.
We traveled to Peru, New Zealand, France.
We bungee-jumped from cliffs, we sipped red wine,

we shopped for clothes that fit us well. We watched
the president announce more funds. We cried.
We were ashamed of our good appetites.
We watched two women kiss outside the door
of our favorite Chinese restaurant.
We talked about adopting kids. We feared
what people thought of us. We bought a house.
We painted the back bedroom red like blood.
We gave less money to the charities.
We found a nice church that accepted us.
The stained glass windows seemed miraculous.
We ate our dinner. We remembered how
we feared their blood, and how we prayed for it
to end. And how it never really did.

Band of Gold

You told me "the lesser-known lesbians"
like Willa Cather and Alice Toklas
who died unremarkable, quiet deaths
never interested you. After all,
who wouldn't drink or pine themselves into
oblivion alone like that, unloved?
The only reason you were homeless was
because you beat up your brother Leon
after he called you a dyke and your folks
threw you out. You painted your nails pink
while you listened to Freda Payne belt out
"Band of Gold" over and over again.
You said she really knew what she was
talking about, because your girlfriend
left you when she found out you had cancer
and it hurt in exactly the same way.
You said your guess was she was probably
queer too, but since it was the seventies
you couldn't sing about another woman
breaking your heart like that. I was there
when you told the surgeon, sure he could
cut them off, but how would he like it if
someone cut off his cock? After you died
alone in your room one night, your mother
showed up with some hash brownies she'd baked you,
which were too sweet and didn't get us high.
The solarium felt like the inside
of emptiness, bright and airless and hot.
She told me that Leon had moved out, and
Freda Payne was a pretty black woman

who could pass for white and whose sister
was a backup singer for the Supremes.
She had a film career that not many
people know about because of that
goddamn song, that whenever you hear it
you understand, whatever love might be,
it abandons us all us, mercilessly.

Primary Care

You, body, bleed, you stink, you interrupt
with plaintive sounds as if we didn't know
you suffer. Dressed in youth, you dazzle me
with your perfection, body: your two knees,
two eyes, two nipples, your fraught symmetries.
O body, even as you age you sing,
you are tender in certain places, you
believe you could be dying. Body, please,
repair yourself once more, bleed and stink,
decay again until, beneath your fragile skin,
I see the outlines of the soul you shield.
You, body, you will come again to me,
I see you naked in the shower, in
the mirror, realize that somehow you
must never die. O body, you are us,
all any of us has when we are lost.
You are immodest; you are honesty.
I see how careful you are when you bleed,
and when you stink it is God's grief we smell.
You, body, weep, you think, you scar as if
to show us our own history, as if
we didn't know. Body bleed, body stink,
remind us that we suffer, yes, remind
us that we must, or else we never lived.

Nude

I enter unexpectedly, and see
your hair cascading white and gray in loose,
long tresses down the full length of your back.
The nurse is bathing you in honeyed light,
when sunrise in the hospital makes all
seem gorgeous, even the gleaming bedpan,
even the scuffed but bright linoleum,
even the faces peering into death.
Your heart is failing, yet you have the strength
to turn, your breasts still the world's nourishment,
your eyes, though I have diagnosed in them
thick cataracts, alight again with youth's
demure, coquettish indignation. "Please,
excuse me, Doctor, I am indisposed!"
For just a moment, as you pull the sheet
to safeguard your imperiled modesty—
your operatic thighs, your blatant hips,
your ruined neck with its distended veins—
I think you are like Goya's ageless nude,
eternal beckoning of human form,
inviolable, innocent, a gift
that both of us acknowledge, knowing that
such love is too sweet ever to be shared.

Not Untrue

Midnight, and he was asking for the score.
He was at a ball game, alive again—
not alone in the hospital, not scared
of dying like this with his mind half-gone.

I watched the clock, which sometimes could seem not
indifferent—sometimes, its face could seem kind—
but the second hand twitched like an insect,
reminding me that there's never more time.

His oxygen hissed, as if it could tell
secrets. The window previewed what was next:
nothing I could see, a perpetual
black emptiness. The nurse quietly knocked;

she grimaced wanly as she smoothed his sheets,
adjusted his iv, and left. He glared
at me, confused again. His voice was weak:
"Your goddamn mother never really cared."

Midnight still, the clock relentlessly read,
beneath which he seemed even smaller now.
"It's 3 to 1, bottom of the ninth, Dad."
Though I didn't know his name, it somehow

seemed forgivable to hold his chapped hand.
"She loved you, Dad. You know she always did."
I'm still not sure if he could understand,
but who can fault me, even if I lied.

On the Wards

I pass you in a hurry, on my way
to where another woman who I know
is dying of a stroke that in the end
is nothing worse than what is killing you.
Same gurney, same bruised arms and mute IV—
you wait for what might be a final test.
It's something in the way you look at me
that makes me realize you have your own
mistakes you think you're paying for, your own
ungrateful kids, your own unspeakable
pain. Yet you look at me, still desperate
for just another human being to
look kindly back at you, to recognize
in you the end is not far off, is not
so unimaginable. Years ago
I watched a patient of mine say goodbye
to life. She was alone like you, alone
like me, she was in agony. She looked
at me, and I, afraid to be the last
thing here on earth she saw, twisted my head
to look away. I almost do the same
to you, afraid you might imagine me
as later you lie dying, but I don't.
Instead, I look at you remorselessly,
the way I hope that someday I am seen,
the way each one deserves to be imagined,
if not restored to health, then spared this grief.

Alternative Medicine

Wednesday afternoon HIV clinic

I. ADVERSE REACTION

"Pray for me," she asks, her head covered in
a polyester scarf. She doesn't hide
herself for shame; she's lost her hair. We think
it was the AZT. She says that through
the walls of all her suffering, she thinks
she hears God's distant voice when her young son
reads from his new storybook. She's so proud
he's learning English. "Pray for him," she asks
before she leaves, "that he may have enough
to bury me in a fine new white dress!"

II. FAILURE TO THRIVE

He weighs less than ninety pounds. Years ago,
he was a bodybuilder. Muscular
and tanned, he looks like someone else back then,
the photograph he shows me faded now.
"You know, even my cock has shriveled up,"
he says. "No one would want to fuck me now."
He undresses very slowly; I count
his ribs while he fumbles with the blue gown.
When I touch him, he avoids my eyes, stares
up at the blank ceiling instead, and cries.

III. LEUKOPENIA

I see him sometimes when I'm walking home.
He holds his children's hands, refuses to

acknowledge me. I know his viral load,
his T cell count, his medication list,
as if these data somehow pinpoint him.
Enveloped in the park's expanse of snow,
his two small children bobbing next to him
like life preservers, I remember that
he's leukopenic. Snow begins to fall
again, innumerable tiny white flakes.

IV. ADVANCED DIRECTIVES

The rescue regimen is failing too.
He lives alone in an AIDS SRO,
once had two little shi-tzu mixes he
was forced to give up—the neighbors complained
about the barking. Not depressed, he says.
Not suicidal. Still taking his meds.
He watches Oprah, gets a hot lunch daily.
I write the orders in his chart. He says
it's funny, since his mother always said
she wished he'd never been born anyway.

V. CARDIOMYOPATHY

He can't tie his shoes anymore because
his feet are so swollen. Denies chest pain
but says his heart aches, whatever that means.
Ejection fraction less than thirty now.
Strange that it keeps progressing, since the meds
have kept his virus undetectable.
He says he doesn't drink, is sober now
for fifteen years. Assessing the edema,
I leave the imprint of my fingertips
anywhere I press down on his taut skin.

VI. RESISTANCE

I think she must be missing doses, since
she hasn't yet disclosed her status to
her husband, who she fears will leave her—or
worse, if he finds out she's positive now.
Good question—he probably exposed her,
but that's not the point. Here's her genotype:
clean, no resistance mutations at all.
Her virus is wild-type, and so she should
suppress on her twice-a-day regimen.
Either that, or she's just not taking it.

VII. IVDU

"I envy you," he says. "You got it all
figured." I stare at the computer screen.
"IVDU. That means I'm on dope, right?
Just an addict, right?" Silently, I type.
"You got to write me a prescription, man.
IVDU? A-I-D-S. That's AIDS.
Can't you just be happy I'm gonna die
and give me my damn prescription?" I try
to hate him, but write "Percocet" instead.
"Now, that didn't hurt much, did it?" he asks.

VIII. UNIVERSAL PRECAUTIONS

You tell me that like me you must wear gloves
at work, restoring precious paintings at
the MFA. Imagining you bent
intently over some scarred masterwork,
I wonder whether your light touch might heal,
but in another sense: I must protect
us all should suddenly you bleed, while you

expose us to the curious infection
of what is possible to know by life's
wounds. Even through my gloves, your skin feels warm.

IX. OPPORTUNISTIC INFECTION

She tells me that her dream involved a cliff—
no, mountain—that she climbed until she reached
its peak. From there, she saw a pristine view:
unending valleys, white-gray glaciers, snow.
The air was thin and she could hardly breathe.
She suddenly began to cough, and blood
poured out of her like song. But in the dream,
she didn't have tuberculosis yet;
she's sure she was infected with a lie,
and inside her, it was the dream that died.

X. ALTERNATIVE MEDICINE

I won't take antiretrovirals, don't
eat processed foods, and remain celibate.
I will take echinacea for a cold—
I wish all medicines came from the earth
and not some toxic lab where they kill rats
with chemicals they claim "treat" HIV.
I exercise six times a week, and pray
to my own God. I believe that someday
we'll find the cure, and I'll be here to say
that one of us survived to celebrate.

Without My White Coat

I'm not a real doc without my white coat.
I could be anyone: this sullen girl,
some homeless person crying to himself,
that addict who thinks he's got HIV.

I could be anyone: this sullen girl
who studies the ink stain on my white coat,
that addict who thinks he gave HIV
to his boyfriend, who sits in my waiting room.

He studies the ink stain on my white coat.
I wonder if he feels dirty, too.
His boyfriend, who sits in my waiting room,
looked up at me hopefully. I regret

my wondering; I feel dirty, too,
a brown-skinned imposter in my white coat.
"Look up," I say unhopefully, regret
the burning light I shine in his dark eyes;

a brown-skinned imposter in a white coat,
I'm half-surprised he follows my commands.
The burning light I shine in his dark eyes
constricts his pupils. When his tears well up,

I'm not surprised: he follows the commands
of human need. My white coat keeps me clean
and strict before my pupil. His tears well up
as carefully I draw his speechless blood.

Of human need, my white coat keeps me clean,
revealing very little of myself.
Carefully, speechlessly, I draw his blood:
a picture of the unseen soul, perhaps.

Revealing very little of myself,
my white coat holds my shape. Stands for something—
a picture of the unseen soul, perhaps.
Perhaps it is the ghost of who I was.

My white coat holds my shape, stands for something
universal—love, healing, peace. I am,
perhaps, a ghost of something that once was.
I wish I could be better than I am.

Universal love, healing peace: I am
the homeless person crying to himself,
wishing I could be better than I am.
I'm not a real doc without my white coat.

The Performance

Wish Bone the cancer clown came up
to BMT today. The kids
lined up in the solarium,
in two squat rows that looked just like
a dozen blighted eggs, bald heads
shining, the sun on them too bright
as if a miracle were near.
He started with some jokes: *What's black
and white and red all over? Knock-
knock? Who's there? Anita. Who?
I need a hug right now!* They laughed
so hard that one of them, the girl
with no platelets, got a nosebleed.
He twisted up balloons to look
like dachshunds and giraffes, then some
odd shape I didn't recognize
which probably was a mistake
but Deb the nurse said could have been
the knot that formed inside her throat
as shamelessly we lapped it up.
The punch arrived, its blobs of pink
and green sherbet melting, like them
not long for this world. As we left
we grabbed some cookies, happy we
could savor what we knew, in spite
of what we hoped, was cruel joy.

What the Dead See

I wonder what the dead see back on earth.
The living play beach volleyball, dine on quiche.
The dead recall the quiet before birth.

The living play: Christmas near the roaring hearth,
feasting on joy, oblivious to ash.
I wonder what the dead see back on earth,

whether they are watching us, full of wrath,
or if instead it is regret, the wish
it weren't so quiet waiting for rebirth.

The living seem forgetful. We are both
voracious and yet limited by flesh.
We wonder if the dead look back at earth

as if our antics were all that were worth
revisiting. We harken to each crash,
afraid to think the quiet before birth

could someday yet engulf us. As will death.
And so the living play and feast and clash,
and wonder what the dead see back on earth.

If they are watching us watch fireworks,
what must concern them is our headlong rush,
how we are only quiet before birth,

how we forget. So merciless is truth
when we have disavowed grace. Hush, then, hush:
Let us ponder the quiet before birth,
let us wonder what the dead see back on earth.

New Poems

Incidental Finding

The sun through green leaf's flesh recalls
the X-ray: inner structures seen
but imprecisely, branching veins
and something like planned avenues
all leading to the source of what
we never cease to seek. Too few,
too momentarily alight,
these chance encounters with the truth.
The X-ray that permitted me
to see both into you and through
(the glowing silhouette of your
soft tissues like the swaddling soul)
still diagnoses it: "a mass,"
the radiologist in me
could not help noting first—and then,
your failing heart, terribly large.

As We Die

My parents gripe about their health. I think
about when I was young, and tried to force
from them an explanation of—what else
could it have been, but death? Back then, the ink

that clotted in my mother's brush was black
as my ungrateful, doubting soul; my father's
huge plush armchair, tilted slightly back, offered
what seemed eternal rest. Their talk is bleak,

their diverticulosis like a pit
that swallows them, their heart disease an ache
these old emotions only aggravate.
I guess I look to them as giants yet,

immortals who know secrets I cannot.
My father, hard of hearing now, reclines
a little farther back; her face now lined
with years of pain, my mother jabs at knots

of garish sunflowers, pretending we
might yet avoid the conversations that
have made their marks on us. Not what I thought—
past death, at last, dreams keep us perfectly.

Hospital Writing Workshop

Arriving late, my clinic having run
past six again, I realize I don't
have cancer, don't have HIV, like them,
these students who are patients, who I lead
in writing exercises, reading poems.
For them, this isn't academic, it's
reality: I ask that they describe
an object right in front of them, to make
it come alive, and one writes about death,
her death, as if by just imagining
the softness of its skin, its panting rush
into her lap, then she might tame it; one
observes instead the love he lost, he's there,
beside him in his gown and wheelchair,
together finally again. I take
a good, long breath; we're quiet as newborns.
The little conference room grows warm, and there
before my eyes, I see that what I thought
unspeakable was more than this, was hope.

"Doctors Lie, May Hide Mistakes"

(*Boston Globe* headline)

That doctors lie, may hide mistakes
should come as no surprise. Of course
the body we must memorize
in fact cannot be trusted, breasts
embarrassing as cheese soufflés
that didn't rise, scuffed knees as dumb
as grief. The very act of touch
is like a lie, the latex gloves
we wear in case of a mistake
protecting us from pulsing blood's
blithe truths. We lie and hide from what
the stethoscope will try to say,
incapable of listening
itself: the heart, mistaken for
the place where the elusive soul
resides, in fact does not repeat
itself. Instead, it cries, "Of course
we must tell lies, and to be human
is this incalculable mistake."

Comfort Measures Only

I'm really not obsessed with how we die.
I checked the chemistries, I weighed the salts:
pretending we're immortal, we don't cry

when inpatients still refuse to defy
the odds. The clock still ticks, the flowers wilt.
I'm really not obsessed with how we die—

it's more this lack of cogent reasons why
we shut ourselves up tightly in dark vaults.
Pretending I'm immortal, I don't cry

as Father Benedict indemnifies
the mourners for our petty sins and faults.
I'm really not obsessed with how we die

or even why, with so much else to try
to fathom. Think about the sea that silts,
pretending it's immortal: do not cry

for all the creatures it has fossilized,
for all the shining cities death unbuilds.
Don't grow obsessed with all that dies;

instead, we must rejoice in rainfall's lies,
the love we make beneath our threadbare quilts,
pretending we're immortal as we cry

with wonder, as in ecstasy we writhe.
Potassium ions do somersaults
while we obsess on if we've really died—

look to the sky, the stars electrified
as if by dreams of wayward astronauts.
I feel so immortal I could cry!

Admit it, finally: Heave your last sigh,
give in to the invidious assault.
I really was obsessed, until I died.
Pretend to be immortal, for once. Cry.

The Chart

Says fifty-four-year-old obese Hispanic
female—I wonder if they mean the one
with long black braids, Peruvian, who sells
tamales at the farmer's market, tells
me I'm too thin, I better eat; or is
she the Dominican with too much rouge
and almond eyes at the dry cleaners who
must have been so beautiful in her youth;
or maybe she's the Cuban lady drunk
on grief who I've seen half-asleep, alone
as if that bench were only hers, the park
her home at last; or else the Mexican
who hoards the littered papers she collects
and says they are her "documents"; if not,
it could be the Colombian drug addict
whose Spanish, even when she's high, is perfect;
or maybe it's the one who never says
exactly where she's from, but who reminds
me of my grandmother, poor but refined,
lace handkerchief balled up in her plump hand,
who died too young from a condition that
some doctor, nose in her chart, overlooked.

Eden

One day, the boy who lived next door began
to eat the flowers in his mother's garden.
He started with the herbs she grew along
the borders: pungent sage and fragrant thyme,
medicinal oregano. Before
too long, sensing he was onto something,
he turned to tasting roses, irises,
and then, as if he doubted he would find
true love, the petals of the daisies, one
by one. By August it got dangerous:
he ate a foxglove plant, which made his heart
skip beats. They rushed him to the hospital
while we prayed hungrily for God's forgiveness,
not recognizing what he really craved
was to be mortal, yet not be cast out
of our delicious earthly paradise.

Complaint

It should be snowing, but instead it's rain.
Disdain
for February everywhere: in trees
whose leaves
long dead cling pointlessly to branches, mud
like dread
half-frozen in the yard, and sky so gray
the day
seems elderly and half-demented. Why
comply
with life's demands, the potholes in the street
entreat,
and why begin again the journey? So
I go,
the hospital, where patients wait, my end.
I tend
an open wound, correct potassium,
give them
the solace no one really ever has
or gives.
Their beating hearts, their husbands' beatings, their
long stares
beyond the cancers they're not beating, all
a wall—
impenetrable. *Hear me*, they implore;
adore
me, let me live. Yet my complaint is hard,
my words
elusive. Suffering, I hate to say,
is grace.

Morbidity and Mortality Rounds

Forgive me, body before me, for this.
Forgive me for my bumbling hands, unschooled
in how to touch: I meant to understand
what fever was, not love. Forgive me for
my stare, but when I look at you, I see
myself laid bare. Forgive me, body, for
what seems like calculation when I take
a breath before I cut you with my knife
because the cancer has to be removed.
Forgive me for not telling you, but I'm
no poet. Please forgive me, please. Forgive
my gloves, my callous greeting, my unease—
you must not realize I just met death
again. Forgive me if I say he looked
impatient. Please, forgive me my despair,
which once seemed more like recompense. Forgive
my greed, forgive me for not having more
to give you than this bitter pill. Forgive:
for this apology, too late, for those
like me whose crimes might seem innocuous
and yet whose cruelty was obvious.
Forgive us for these sins. Forgive me, please,
for my confusing heart that sounds so much
like yours. Forgive me for the night, when I
sleep too, beside you under the same moon.
Forgive me for my dreams, for my rough knees,
for giving up too soon. Forgive me, please,
for losing you, unable to forgive.

Diagnosis Code

I spoke to her fever, and it replied
that no, it would not come down, that it liked
its nearness to the blazing sun. I laughed

with her delusion, watching from inside
our semiprivate room, as doctors lurked
behind their big computers making graphs

of those who lived, and those who slowly died.
I drank a glass of wine with one who looked
like he could use some company, one-half

of his left lung missing; cancer aside,
he seemed the picture of good health. *As luck
would have it*, read the cheerful epitaph.

I couldn't help but feel that I had cried.
The doctor watched his timepiece as it clicked,
another second gone. Another gaffe

the politician made, a truth belied:
Fix Medicare, cut Medicaid! We lack
the promised cure; the snake writhes up the staff.

Ancient Mythologies of Healing

Whatever most afflicted them—the pain
of kidney stones or gout, the blindness caused
by syphilis or cataracts, the loss
of limbs from gangrene—it was plain

to them the cause of illness. Who but gods
could turn clear urine into blood, take sight
by day yet send prophetic dreams at night,
change brave Achilles' heel to stinking mud?

Because they were incapable of fault,
the gods expressed their perverse willingness
to let the misery they wrought seem less
by having offspring whose disdain was felt

inside us differently. Apollo gave
the Muses their ability to soothe our souls—
Euterpe's flute, useless but to console,
Erato's lyre, able to revive

even the most despondent warrior.
Today, we graph the music of the heart
and suffer poetry as if it hurt,
yet understand no more of gods or cures.

Treponema Pallidum

How I could only wish I knew romance
first time I saw it through the microscope;
what corkscrewing, what so beguiling dance
against the dark, as if so full of hope

it wouldn't seem like just desire could blind
us to the truth. I looked at him convinced
my heart would burst. Of course I felt ashamed,
because the doctor only knows, not loves,

because I almost missed the diagnosis.
He stood there naked, marked, as if instead
he waited to be judged. The rash ran over
his palms and soles like something close to dread

and yet I couldn't stop imagining
that ecstasy was worth what price he paid,
the starched white coat that showed my distancing
a purity I'd sacrifice for pain.

Just Know Your Shit

I want a doctor who just knows his shit.
Don't hold my hand when my heart fibrillates—

just shock me with the right amount of juice.
Don't hold my hand, just check my thready pulse,

be sure my calcium is adequate.
Don't ask me what I think, just tell me that

it's not life-threatening, we have a cure.
Just tell me that you don't have time to care,

you have to cut me open now, before
it kills me. Don't imagine how the scar

will throb, don't hold my hand. Just tell me that
the odds are terrible, but if you're right

another round of chemotherapy
might help. I want a doctor who is free

to do whatever must be done, who sees
it's bad but doesn't flinch, ignoring me

when he decides what he'll do next, who knows
his shit. Don't hold my hand when my mind goes,

there's always something you can fix. For God's
sake, don't feel for me. Just do it, don't sob.

Hippocratic Oath 2.0

The doctor may reserve the right to do
some harm. He may not pray for you. He might
consider other interventions like
expressing his regret or wishing he
felt something in his heart besides his fear.
The doctor may excuse himself when you
start talking late at night about your pain,
your daughter's disappointing choice of husband,
or what the end of all this torture is.
The doctor must refuse to put himself
before his patients' needs, nor profit from
the wisdom they dispense when staring at
the bruises on their arms from their ivs.
The doctor may reserve the right to ask
forgiveness should he comprehend that life
is short, is precious. After, he is free
to swear, to drink his coffee strong and black.
The doctor may kick back and think of you,
reflecting on his day poisonously.
He may seek solace from the rhythmic bleeps
of his machines, reminding him that life
is fragile, is a gift. The doctor may
reserve the right to look away, but he
must always recognize it was his voice
that made this harmless, sacred pledge, for you.

On the Beauty of Science

A colleague at my hospital has won
a major prize, for seminal research
into the role of lipid bodies in
the eosinophil. How I once loved
the eosinophil, its nucleus
contorted, cytoplasm flecked with red.
Of course, I wondered at its function, why
it self-destructed on encountering
some allergen or parasitic egg, how
it killed by dying. Now we know so much
that joy in the mysterious seems quaint.
Its valentine to us undone by thought,
the blushing eosinophil explained:
embarrassed by its smallness, or enraged
that all its selflessness should be betrayed.

Poem for Ebola

The neighbors' sprinkler system hissed, as if
the decontamination process were
beginning. Pouring bleach, I dreamed how white
my dirty laundry, sanitized and fresh,
could be. The neighbors' African au pair
hosed down their driveway while the twin girls laughed.
I turned the compost, saw its fat worms twist.
The neighbors' television flashed with those
meek forms, their masks, unable to escape.
I found a dead bird near the kitchen window;
its beady eyes were rimmed with blood, its wings
fanned out like feathers in a fancy hat.
I thought of when the neighbors' son had died
of AIDS, of how it seemed the news had come
on black wings silently descending on
October's haunted winds. I swept the deck,
the neighbors' fence defending its domain,
then fertilized the lawn, my rubber gloves
protecting me, my fear not gone, still here
like anything that spreads and lives forever.

Invaders

She says that back in Mexico the map
of the United States that hung above
the teacher's desk was like a floating island
impossible to reach, impossible

for any girl like her to even dream
might welcome her. She gazes now instead
above my desk, her flattened breasts a map
no more accessible, no more forgiving,

the spreading cancer numinous, one could
say even beautiful, deceptive as
that distant promise. Here just one short year,
she tells me of the landlord calling them

"invaders," six of them who shared a room,
the only toilet down the hall. She says
she cried alone beneath the Virgin Mary,
the church the only place she knew to go,

the flickering of candles casting shadows
in shapes above her everywhere like maps
to other worlds; she says she prayed for this
to be a better world. The clinic throbs

in pain outside my door, so many dreams
deferred, so many hearts invaded by
resentment or remorse, so many seas traversed
and borders crossed. So many journeys done.

Metastatic Colon Cancer

I visit him before I head back home.
While we make small talk, on the television
Maria Sharapova battles to
survive, to make it to the semifinals.
It's winter here, but on the screen it's summer;
Australians get sunburned watching her.
Maria Sharapova runs down balls;
she screams so loudly after every hit
it sounds like she is giving birth. My patient
frowns, asks the nurse to bring a popsicle.
He watches her, wishing for her forehand
to hold strong, wishing he was in Australia.
Maria Sharapova screams again,
her sweat bejeweling her, as if she could
be somehow more beautiful, more alive.
Her sneakers squeak as she refuses to
give up, relentless as she chases down
another ball. My patient watches her
accelerate across the court, so sure,
so full of life it seems untrue. She screams
and hits a winner down the line. The crowd
erupts; Maria Sharapova cries.
It is like beauty crying; it is painful.
I say goodbye too awkwardly; he cries
because we know this visit is our last.

Cardiology

When we first met, my heart pounded. They said
the shock of it was probably what broke
his heart. In search of peace, we traveled once
to Finland, tasted reindeer heart. It seemed
so heartless, how you wanted it to end.
I noticed on the nurse who took his pulse
a heart tattooed above her collarbone.
The kids played hearts all night to pass the time.
You said that at its heart rejection was
impossible to understand. "We send
our heartfelt sympathy," was written in
the card your mother sent, in flowing script.
I tried interpreting his EKG,
which looked like knife wounds to the heart. I knew
enough to guess he wouldn't last much longer.
As if we'd learned our lines by heart, you said,
"I can't explain." "Please don't," was my reply.
They say the heart is just a muscle. Or
the heart is where the human soul resides.
I saw myself in you; you looked so much
like him. You didn't have the heart to say
you didn't need me anymore. I still
can see that plastic statue: Jesus Christ,
his sacred heart aflame, held out in his
own hands. He finally let go. A grief
this great is borne, not felt. Borne in the heart.

I Imagine Again I Don't Let You Die

This time, I think I got it right:
I know it was a dream, I know
I was asleep, and yet the night

receded. Sky was indigo.
This time, I told you everything,
and somehow, you remained aglow,

the setting sun unsettling
in turning you to oranges
and golds. I think I walked along

beside you for a while; I guess
I made you laugh, though I forget
your smile, and I forget my jest.

Too soon, this time, too soon. Regret
came over me; I never said
how much I love you. Toward which debt

could such a loss be credited?
Next time, I know I'll get it right.
I'll dream that you are never dead,

and that beneath this purple light
and past the sun as red as blood,
I'll hold you close, I'll get it right.

Swim for Life

for Mary Fisher

Crowds throng the creaking boardwalk to sign up
to swim from Long Point back to Provincetown,
a fund-raiser for AIDS and women's groups.
Three seagulls levitate, then spiral down.
The atmosphere is festive, jovial,
a touch irreverent—we're all still here,
the sun is glorious, and after all,
these aging men in Speedos bear the scars,
these women in their wet suits just as brave.
Old disco anthems pulsate as they stretch
and limber up, the glittering of waves
that lap in time along the pebbled beach
a drag queen's overdone green eye shadow.
A stiff breeze riffles through the many names
on prayer ribbons draped above: "For Joe,"
I glimpse on one; "I miss you, Mary Jane,"
entreats another. Soon, it's time. I watch
the swimmers gather, board the launches, fade
to tiny dots, like drifts of stars just out of reach,
like friendships that were suddenly unmade,
like memories we never thought we'd have.
The ocean swallows them. We're quiet, stunned
by what heroic acts can still achieve:
from death, reclaim what's human, save what's loved.

Your Poems Are Never Joyful

Why not? A line or two that celebrates
the joy you felt when you awoke to find

yourself alive, the beeper summoning
you not to your own death, but to a thing

you could not comprehend. And what is joy
if not the recognition of good luck,

how lucky you were, though you too were gay,
not to be sick. Why not recall the Haight,

why not recall how much he loved to "frolic,"
his small apartment opening your mind

to possibilities you hadn't let
yourself admit. The opposite of weight,

perhaps, is joy. Remember how it weighed
on you, that even though you thrived,

that even though you laughed with friends about
the ill-spelled entrées at the Chinese dive

("moo goo guy pen," the knowing menu said,
and "eggs few young," as if it understood

repressed young doctors' lack of social lives)—
that though you felt so free on coming out,

he stayed there, dying. See the awful blood
his cough produced; recall how you felt glad

it wasn't you. Weeks later, underneath
sequoias, centuries turned into wood,

you cried for him, but then you smiled.
You finally could make some sense of death.

You hiked alone, comforted by mourning doves,
and felt the joy in each hard breath, each long mile.

Addiction

Do trees crave sunshine? Could the neighbors' boy
not live without his dreams of paradise?
I'd watch him peering out his window, sky

above him blue and innocent, like it
might really break his fall. I promised that
I'd never touch the stuff again, but light

has this way of lying to you, betraying
you, telling you your mind is not decaying.
That you're not really crazy to be seeing

things, beauty maybe, maybe even hope.
"I need to get my hands on some good dope,"
he said, while elsewhere in the ER hips

or sometimes hearts lay broken. Suffering
is just we're always seeking one damn thing.
Call it what you will: addiction, the song

of the sirens, or whatever else it is
we somehow lost. Like night aches for stars, this
sharp needle yearns for awful bliss.

Post-Emergency

Regret is what I feel the most.
I've not lived well, despite my health.
I think of them, unwilling hosts
to deadly pathogens whose stealth

was literally breathtaking
(the chest X-rays I tried to read
while they were wracked by cough: words ring
all night inside my thoughtless head;

"ground-glass opacities," I think,
and "increased interstitial markings").
Two decades past and I still drink
the ironies of their dark blood, sing

the old songs of their respirators.
Not feeling is what I regret.
My stethoscope, co-conspirator,
drapes itself around my neck,

as if it could console as yet
I make my rounds. I've not lived well
these intervening years, beset
by memories a kind of hell

has left imprinted on my brain.
I tried to write but poetry
would not suffice, could not explain
their elevated LFTs,

emaciated faces like
the clocks that ticked above their beds,
expressionless. A fever spikes,
a spent IV alarms; the dead

who haunt these wards are everywhere.
Young hustlers still get PCP;
a man my age has lost his hair
to treatment for lymphoma. We

forget how awful it once was,
implore each other silently
if not to speak, then surely rise
again to meet the day. I see

the nurses bathing them, and hope
that comfort isn't all we crave
when life recedes and we must grope
for what it meant. Let us be saved

unwittingly as shoppers at
the mall, where no gunman goes crazed
because he realizes that
we're innocent; let us be saved

as much by wishing we could be
alive again, but better than
we were—regretful, yes, but free
of guilt, in love that was not wrong.

Lessons Not Learned during Medical Training

His father said that when he told him, it was like treason.
We guessed it would be over soon, after we trach'ed him.
I learned the procedure: *See one, do one, teach one.*
The stars decorating the parking lot seemed to be thinking
as I left the hospital; when something somewhere was taken,
an alarm went off. I remember he joked he felt turned on
when he undressed in my exam room. I thought, it's sacred,
this time we have on earth, as they gave out tokens
(lapel pins with his picture) at the funeral. Leaves talking
in trees, in the sweet breeze that seemed to be mistaken,
beneath a sun that hadn't lost its faith in God. Try not
to cry, I said to myself, but no one heard me. It took him
years to come out, he told me, and he'd tried once
to kill himself before. He said he knew it sounded trite, but
he always fell for messed-up, married, probably straight guys.
I liked one of the med-surg nurses, or so I pretended.
His sister flipped through *People* at his bedside. Trains run
on time as they always do, and life becomes tiresome.
As his mother read a poem, I wished I could trade me
for him. I try to picture his green eyes, ear-to-ear grin;
I see my own face in his open coffin. When the tears come
they warn us not to feel anything, but I betray them.

Quatrains from the Clinic

They wait for me—in wheelchairs, painfully,
or sometimes I imagine scared, or high
because they cannot bear it, naked thighs
exposed by paper gowns. They wait for me

while reading pamphlets on mammography,
or tattered, long-outdated magazines,
or maybe just the posters for vaccines
that promise if they follow what we say

they might live longer, long enough at least.
They wait for me, their palpitations racing,
their ghostly blood pressures silently rising,
their stomachs grumbling since they're told to fast,

their headaches like a sledgehammer. They wait
for me, their vision blurred, their hearing lost,
their appetites diminished. Baring breasts,
assessing wounds, I know that I'm too late.

End of Life Discussion

She speaks for him, her husband's deepening
dementia like a river through which she
has led him to this place, its current strong
but not unconquerable. Carefully,

she holds his hand, still guiding him as in
Korean now the translator explains
what I have said. Stiff-backed, his peaceful grin
a mask that tries to hide the tumor's pain,

he sits as if imagining he sees
her face beyond a soundless waterfall,
through mist that moistens his unblinking eyes.
His wife says, "Doctor, sorry, is that all?"

The Pond

We've come for many reasons. Some will swim,
some hike along the trails. The divorcées
in spandex pants, made up and coiffed, look glum.
A couple tend to their disabled daughter.
The pond reflects us all, although the water
is coated with a golden scum of pollen.
I'm almost halfway round it, feeling sullen;
you float awhile, then dive, as if to say

that any one of us might vanish, just
like that. Meanwhile, the pond endures, the birds
keep foraging, the sun glares as it must.
I hold my breath and try to meditate,
to summon forth some words Thoreau once wrote,
but I'm distracted by the traffic's roar
and plastic bottles littering the shore.
The world wants to be beautiful, unmarred

by what we do and think, yet here we are.
We yearn to be alone but can't, we crave
the perfect antidote, the painless cure.
The helmeted young men on bicycles
whiz past, our flaws still inescapable.
Just then, you break the surface with a splash
then paddle aimlessly, bare skin a flash
of white in so much murk, until the waves

you make are lapping at my toes. Two women
smooth out a towel farther down the beach;
their kiss describes what else we have in common.

Her T-shirt blazoned with a prancing fairy,
their girl's wheelchair is only temporary;
the broken hearts and the unending races
are borne here, in this briefest of embraces.
You cross the pond—far, yet still within reach.

Hospice Rounds

One looks at me as from a distance.
Another does not cry; "It's only pain,"
she says, as if cancer were just a nuisance
one looks at square, from a distance.
Outside the window, sunshine, like persistence.
Yet how Bach from the radio seems like rain.
She looks at me. From this great distance
I'm another who cannot cry. Or feel pain.

Ghazal: By the Sea

for Kim Bridgford

We always wanted a house by the sea.
A place to grow old together, by the sea.

My father's house, in Guantánamo, stolen.
He still tastes *arroz con cangrejo*, served by the sea.

That whitewashed house in Greece, perched on a bluff,
dream home to tourists. Views of migrants, drowned by the sea.

Those hovels in Mexico turned into condos.
No fisherman left to be nourished by the sea.

We looked into the Maldives, imagined a paradise
slowly vanishing, sands swallowed by the sea.

Poets love islands—as if only love, and not war,
can be so utterly surrounded by the sea.

Yet the wars continue: in the West Bank
a child blown to bits, playing by the sea.

What else to do but imagine flight, the respite
of seagulls, their harmless dive-bombing. By the sea,

it almost seems possible change is near.
Our greed seems small when we stroll by the sea,

even innocent. In rainbow leis, once we took vows
that seemed to rhyme with the palms by the sea;

a luckier child builds sandcastles, and buries
his uncles up to their necks by the sea.

The cottage in Provincetown, bought in foreclosure.
Its last owners dead of AIDS, in graves by the sea.

Today, we rest on the beach, dreaming our silly
dreams. We accept the lies made up by the sea.

We look to the horizon; behind us, beyond the dunes,
a field gathers dew. Waves lap. We end and begin by the sea.

The Stethoscope Replies

I've heard this one so many times before:
the story of some awful heartbreak, or
the murmuring of love found at long last.
A breath is held, while silently the pain
returns; the scratching of the tiny crab
too many years of smoking left behind.
I've heard it all before, the agony
of drowning in the flood of one's own blood
that slowly rises from some inner wound;
the barking cough that proves we're animal.
They press me to your chest, so I can hear
it all, the song of the alveoli's
end-expiratory, musical wheeze,
the sinister, if not ironic rub.
I've heard it countless times before.
Even the sound of sobbing, so plain
it surely doesn't need my amplifying,
though still you try to speak, even when the tube
(I know by checking breath sounds afterward)
is placed. I've heard it all before, the ebb
and flow of life, the pure monotony
of wanting somehow to express the wish,
the need to live. I touch you silently,
and listen, nestled in your wrinkled breasts,
or at the angle of your jaw, so cold
in my unspeakable amazement.
Inhale, exhale. I've heard it all before.